with
Matt Green

THE
RAPPING
SCIENCE
TEACHER

From the author:

To my incredible wife, Helen – there would be no science raps without you. Thank you for being my constant encourager, for believing in me from the very beginning, and for giving me that first push to step in front of the camera. You are, and always have been, my number one supporter. Huge thanks to my mum and dad for instilling in me the value of education and shaping my path to becoming a teacher, and to my wonderful in-laws, Emma and Mike, for your unwavering support. My heartfelt gratitude goes to my management, Wendy Woolfson Talent and PR, for creating this incredible publishing opportunity. Wendy and Hannah – your inspiring work and guidance turn my dreams into reality.
Finally, thank you to DK for believing in this project and bringing it to life.

Author Matt Green, The Rapping Science Teacher
Author Contributor Jim Newall

Produced for DK by
Editorial Just Content Limited
Design Fourth Wall

Senior Editor Amelia Jones
Managing Editor Katherine Neep
Managing Art Editors Sarah Corcoran, Elizabeth Arnoux
Pre-Production Designer Rohit Singh
Senior Production Controller Meskerem Berhane
Publisher Sarah Forbes
Managing Director, Learning Hilary Fine

First published in Great Britain in 2026 by
Dorling Kindersley Limited
20 Vauxhall Bridge Road,
London SW1V 2SA

The authorised representative in the EEA is
Dorling Kindersley Verlag GmbH. Arnulfstr. 124,
80636 Munich, Germany

Lyrics copyright © Matt Green 2026
Matt Green has asserted his right to be identified as the author of the lyrics in this work
Text and design copyright © 2026 Dorling Kindersley Limited
A Penguin Random House Company
10 9 8 7 6 5 4 3 2 1
001–352649-Jan/2026

All rights reserved.
No part of this publication may be reproduced, stored in or introduced into a retrieval system, or transmitted, in any form, or by any means (electronic, mechanical, photocopying, recording, or otherwise), without the prior written permission of the copyright owner. DK values and supports copyright. Thank you for respecting intellectual property laws by not reproducing, scanning or distributing any part of this publication by any means without permission. By purchasing an authorised edition, you are supporting writers and artists and enabling DK to continue to publish books that inform and inspire readers. No part of this publication may be used or reproduced in any manner for the purpose of training artificial intelligence technologies or systems. In accordance with Article 4(3) of the DSM Directive 2019/790, DK expressly reserves this work from the text and data mining exception.

A CIP catalogue record for this book is available from the British Library.
ISBN: 978-0-2417-7160-0

Printed and bound in China

www.dk.com

This book was made with Forest Stewardship Council™ certified paper – one small step in DK's commitment to a sustainable future. Learn more at www.dk.com/uk/information/sustainability

Welcome from Matt

Welcome to Rapping up Physics – by me, Matt Green The Rapping Science Teacher!

This book takes everything I've learnt from all my years of teaching in schools and on social media and lays it out in an easy-to-use revision format.

Helping students to understand science means a huge amount to me, so I have put blood, sweat and tears into this guide to make Physics revision not just simple, but unforgettable.

First, read each topic section to understand the key ideas. Then move to the RAPPING UP! section to lock it in with a short, punchy rap that makes the facts stick.

Forget boring textbooks – this guide is your secret weapon, designed to help you master GCSE Physics and walk into your exams with total confidence.

Let's drop the beat and start learning.
Rap. Revise. Remember!

Matt

Contents

Energy — 5
Energy Stores and Systems 6
Changes in Energy 8
Energy Changes in Systems 10
Power 12
Energy Transfers in a System 14
National and Global Energy Resources ... 16
Brain Booster 18

Electricity — 19
Circuits, Charge and Current 20
Current, Resistance and Potential Difference 22
Resistors 24
Series and Parallel Circuits 26
Domestic Uses and Safety 28
Energy Transfers 30
Static Electricity 32
Brain Booster 34

Particle Model of Matter — 35
Density and States of Matter 36
Changes of State and Internal Energy 38
Energy Transfers 40
Particle Model and Pressure 42
Brain Booster 44

Atomic Structure — 45
Models of the Atom 46
Atoms and Isotopes 48
Reactive Decay and Nuclear Radiation ... 50
Half-life and Contamination 52
Hazards and Uses of Radiation 54
Nuclear Fission and Fusion 56
Brain Booster 58

Forces — 59
Forces and their Interactions 60
Resultant Forces and Work Done 62
Forces and Elasticity 64
Moments, Levers and Gears 66
Pressure in a Fluid 68
Distance, Displacement and Speed 70
Velocity and Distance–Time Graphs 72
Acceleration 74
Newton's Laws of Motion 76
Forces and Braking 78
Braking Distance 80
Brain Booster 82

Waves — 83
Properties of Waves 84
Measuring the Speed of Waves 86
Reflection and Refraction 88
Electromagnetic Waves 90
Uses, Hazards and Visible Light 92
Lenses 94
Brain Booster 96

Magnetism and Electromagnetism — 97
Magnetism 98
Electromagnetism 100
Brain Booster 102

Space Physics — 103
The Solar System and Stars 104
Orbital Motion and Red-shift 106
Brain Booster 108

Answers 109
Exam Board References 111
Acknowledgments 112

Energy

At the end of this chapter, you should be able to:

- ✓ Recall the energy stores and the ways energy can be transferred.
- ✓ Describe changes in energy stores when a system changes.
- ✓ Recall and use the equations for kinetic energy, elastic potential energy and gravitational potential energy.
- ✓ Define the term "specific heat capacity".
- ✓ Know how to determine the specific heat capacity of a material.
- ✓ Define and calculate power.
- ✓ Recall and apply the principle of conservation of energy.
- ✓ Describe unwanted energy transfers and ways of reducing them.
- ✓ Calculate efficiency.
- ✓ Describe the main renewable and non-renewable energy resources.
- ✓ Compare ways energy resources are used.
- ✓ Explain why some energy resources are more reliable than others.

Energy Stores and Systems

Key facts

- A system is an object or a group of objects.
- The main ways in which energy can be stored are: kinetic, thermal, chemical, gravitational potential, elastic potential, magnetic, electrostatic, and nuclear.
- Energy is transferred from one store to another when a system changes.

Ways energy is stored

Kinetic: stored by a moving object.

Thermal: a block of ice stores less thermal energy than a bar of chocolate that is at room temperature.

Chemical: the chemical bonds between molecules store energy.

Gravitational potential: an object raised 50 m above the ground stores more gravitational energy than the same object raised 10 m above the ground.

Elastic potential: a stretched spring stores more elastic potential energy than the same spring when it is not stretched.

Magnetic: there is energy between the poles of two magnets, whether they are attracting or repelling each other.

Electrostatic: charged particles store energy.

Nuclear: the nucleus of an atom stores energy.

Energy can be transferred from one store to another by:

- Heating.
- Work done by forces.
- Work done when a current flows (by electricity).
- Electromagnetic radiation (such as light) and mechanical radiation (such as sound).

RAPPING UP!

This topic you can't avoid.
Just like **money**, if you're employed,
It's transferred or it's enjoyed.
It can't be made, can't be destroyed.

Don't like me?
You ain't seen a teacher like me in your life.
We covering stores. We measure in **joules**.
Let's go through all the types.

Movement's **kinetic**, heat's thermal.
There are a few more I can list in full.
Seven are straight, two potential:
Elastic and gravitational.

I'll keep the rest short and I'll keep it sweet.
The **energy** types they all describe me.
I come with that fire, I come with that heat.
I got a sound mind and I'm light on my feet.

Magnetic, **electricity**.
My bars are like iron, I shock when I speak.
Teacher oops, don't want it with me.
They drop to the floor like gravity.

Just two left, I'll say what these are:
Chemical energy and **nuclear**.
Before I leave here I got something to say.
The unit is **joule** and the symbol is J.

Ways energy is transferred

When a pendulum swings

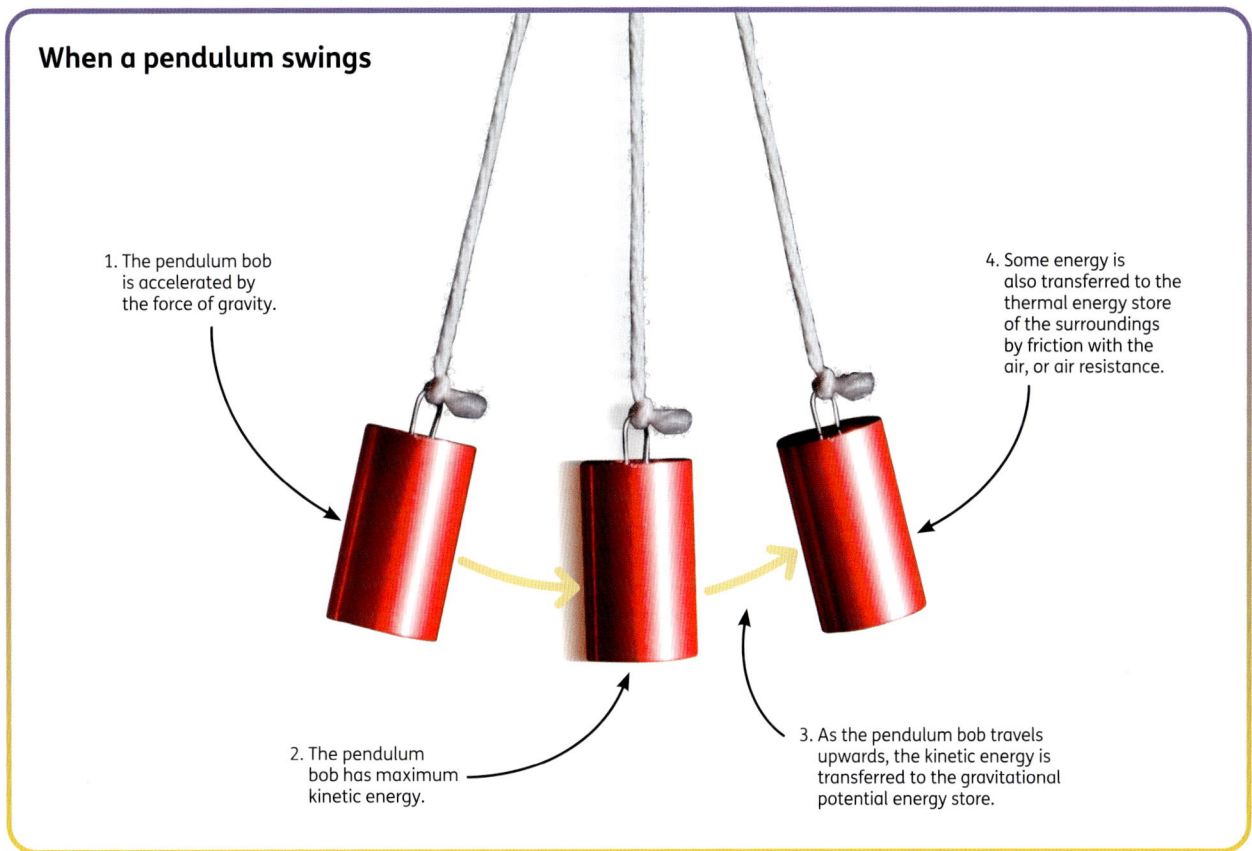

1. The pendulum bob is accelerated by the force of gravity.
2. The pendulum bob has maximum kinetic energy.
3. As the pendulum bob travels upwards, the kinetic energy is transferred to the gravitational potential energy store.
4. Some energy is also transferred to the thermal energy store of the surroundings by friction with the air, or air resistance.

When a car slows down

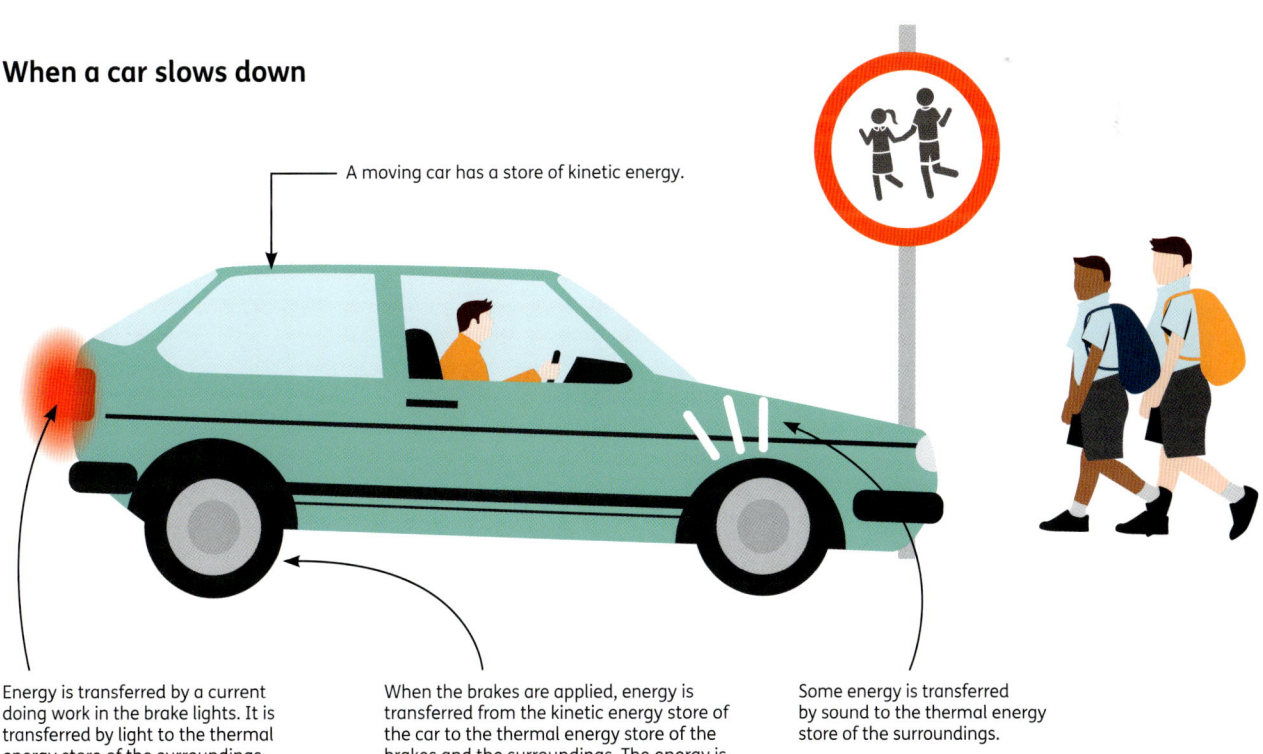

A moving car has a store of kinetic energy.

Energy is transferred by a current doing work in the brake lights. It is transferred by light to the thermal energy store of the surroundings.

When the brakes are applied, energy is transferred from the kinetic energy store of the car to the thermal energy store of the brakes and the surroundings. The energy is transferred by the force applied by the brakes.

Some energy is transferred by sound to the thermal energy store of the surroundings.

Energy

Changes in Energy

Key facts

- An object has more kinetic energy if it moves faster or gains mass.
- Kinetic energy (in J) = 0.5 × Mass (in kg) × (Speed (in m/s))²
- Elastic potential energy (in J) = 0.5 × Spring constant (in N/m) × (Extension (in m))²
- An object has more gravitational potential energy if it moves up from the surface or gains mass.
- Change in gravitational potential energy (in J) =
  Mass (in kg) × Gravitational field strength (in N/kg) × Change in vertical height (in m)

RAPPING UP!

Kinetic goes up if you gain more speed,
Or if the mass grows — that's all you need.

The formula's simple, don't be scared
Half times mass times the **speed squared**.

Elastic potential's got a **formula** trust
When **springs** get stretched, energy goes up.

Half times **k**, times **e** squared.
Starts in metres, be prepared.

Gravitational energy goes up with height,
Mass and field strength you heard me right.

Times them all together then what you have,
is the **GPE** – now thats a rap.

Energy and roller coasters

As a roller coaster travels along, energy transfers between its kinetic energy (KE) store and gravitational potential energy (GPE) store.

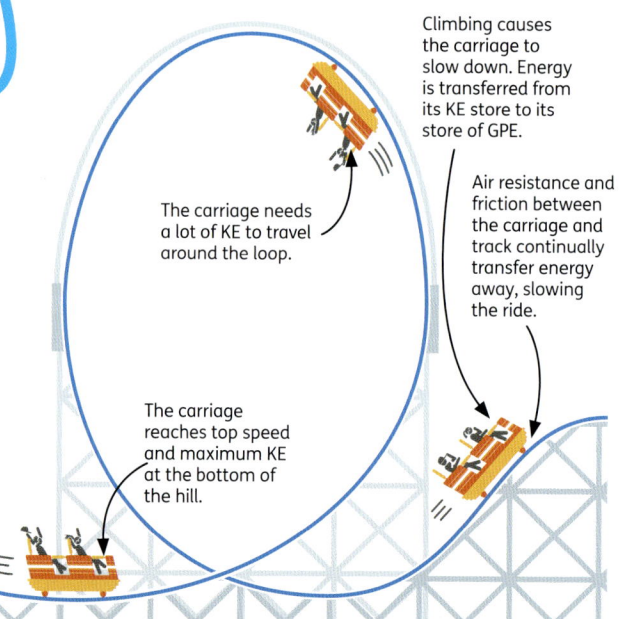

Climbing causes the carriage to slow down. Energy is transferred from its KE store to its store of GPE.

The carriage needs a lot of KE to travel around the loop.

Air resistance and friction between the carriage and track continually transfer energy away, slowing the ride.

The carriage reaches top speed and maximum KE at the bottom of the hill.

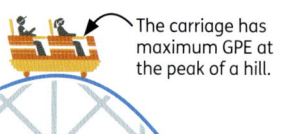

The carriage has maximum GPE at the peak of a hill.

As the carriage goes downhill, GPE is transferred to KE and it speeds up.

Energy

Maths skills

When numbers get very large, there are prefixes you can use.
- k means kilo, or 1,000 or 10^3. 1,000 J = 1 kJ
- M means mega, or 1,000,000 or 10^6. 1,000,000 J = 1M J = 1,000 kJ
- G means giga, or 1,000,000,000 or 10^9. 1,000,000,000 J = 1G J = 1000 MJ = 1,000,000 kJ

Calculating gravitational potential energy

Question
A crane lifts a pallet of bricks to a height of 25 m. The pallet has a mass of 2,000 kg.

The gravitational field strength is 10 N/kg.

Calculate the change in gravitational potential energy of the pallet of bricks.

Answer
Change in gravitational potential energy = Mass × Gravitational field strength × Change in vertical height

= 2,000 × 10 × 25
= 500,000 J or 500 kJ

Calculating elastic potential energy

Question
A spring is stretched by 15 cm. The spring constant of the spring is 400 N/m.

Answer
Convert extension to metres:

15 cm = 0.15 m

Elastic potential energy = 0.5 × Spring constant × (Extension)^2

= 0.5 × 400 × 0.15^2

= 4.5 J

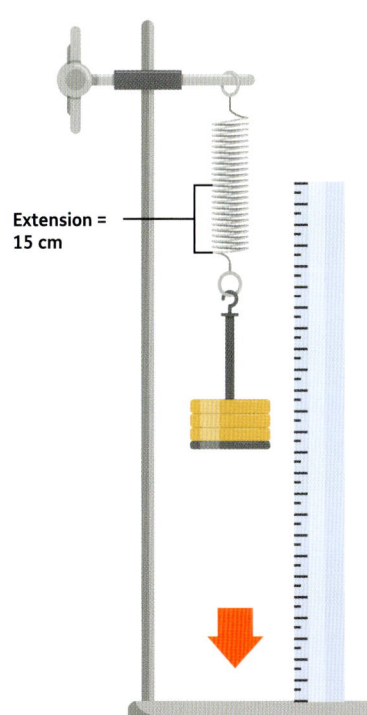

Energy Changes in Systems

Key facts

- Change in thermal energy (in J) =
  Mass (in kg) × Specific heat capacity (in J/kg °C) × Temperature change (in °C)
- The specific heat capacity of a substance is the amount of energy required to raise the temperature of 1 kilogram of the substance by 1 degree Celsius.

Specific heat capacity

The amount of energy needed to raise the temperature by 1°C depends on the substance. The graph shows how the specific heat capacity varies for some common materials.

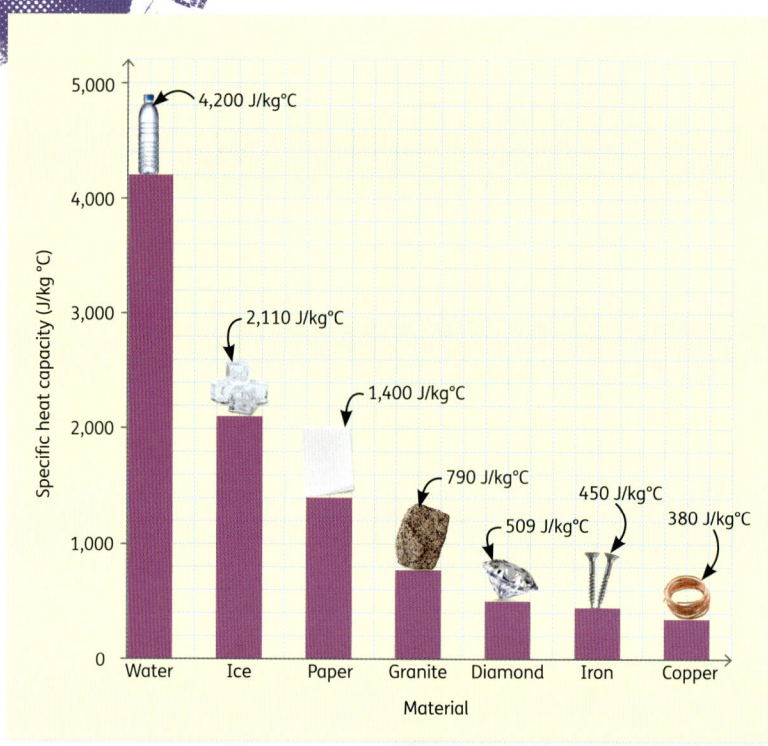

RAPPING UP!

Thermal energy, let's get this done.
Times mass by change in temp, that's **ONE**.
TWO - Times that by the SHC.
That's specific heat capacity.
It's in **joules per kilo** per degree.
Water's one is high you'll see.
4,200 – wanna know why?
It takes **more heat** just to make it rise,
Compared to metals or ice!

Calculating change in thermal energy

Question
A cup holds 350 g (0.35 kg) of tea. The tap water used to brew the tea was at 5°C. The specific heat capacity of water is 4,200 J/kg °C.

How much energy is needed to bring the water to make a cup of tea to boiling point?

Answer
Change in temperature = 100 − 5 = 95°C

Change mass to kg: 350 g = 0.35 kg

Change in thermal energy =
Mass × Specific heat capacity ×
Temperature change

= 0.35 × 4,200 × 95

= 139,650 J (139.65 kJ)

Question
The temperature of a block of aluminium increases from 20°C to 50°C. The mass of the block is 750 g. The specific heat capacity of aluminium is 900 J/kg °C.

Calculate the change in the thermal energy store of the aluminium block.

Answer
Change in temperature = 50 − 20 = 30°C

Change mass to kg: 750 g = 0.75 kg

Change in thermal energy =
Mass × Specific heat capacity ×
Temperature change

= 0.75 × 900 × 30

= 20,250 J

Science skills

Determining specific heat capacity
You can use the equipment shown in the diagram to measure the temperature rise of the aluminium cylinder and the amount of energy transferred to it.

You can then use the equation to calculate the specific heat capacity of the aluminium.

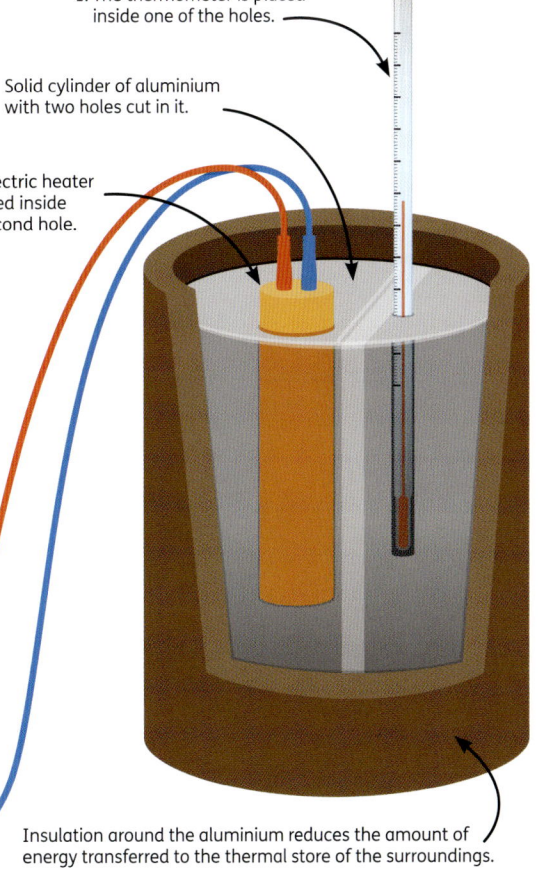

1. The thermometer is placed inside one of the holes.

Solid cylinder of aluminium with two holes cut in it.

2. The electric heater is placed inside the second hole.

3. The metal is heated for 10 minutes.

4. Use a joulemeter to measure the amount of energy transferred.

Insulation around the aluminium reduces the amount of energy transferred to the thermal store of the surroundings.

Energy

Power

Key facts

- Power is defined as the rate at which energy is transferred or the rate at which work is done.
- An energy transfer of 1 joule per second is equal to 1 watt of power.
- Power (in W) = $\dfrac{\text{Energy transferred (in J)}}{\text{Time (in s)}}$
- Power (in W) = $\dfrac{\text{Energy work done (in J)}}{\text{Time (in s)}}$

Work done

Remember, **work done** = energy transferred. See page 62 for more on work done.

Question
A person pushes a box along the floor. The person does 150 J of work on the box in 4 seconds.

Calculate the person's power.

Answer
Power = $\dfrac{\text{Work done}}{\text{Time}}$

= $\dfrac{150}{4}$

= 37.5 W

Calculating power

Question
A boy weighing 350 newtons climbs 2 m up a ladder in 5 seconds. He does 700 J of work. Calculate his power.

Answer
Power = $\dfrac{\text{Energy transferred}}{\text{Time}}$

= $\dfrac{700}{5}$

= 140 W

Question
A hairdryer transfers 180 kJ of energy in 2 minutes. Calculate the power of the hairdryer.

Answer
First change time to seconds:

Time = 2 min = 2 × 60 = 120 seconds

Then change energy to joules:

Energy = 180 kJ = 180,000 J

Then use the equation:

Power = $\dfrac{\text{Energy transferred}}{\text{Time}}$

= $\dfrac{180,000}{120}$

= 1,500 W or 1.5 kW

Maths skills

Using standard form
A number in **standard form** is given as:

$A \times 10^n$

- A number between 1 and 10.
- Power of 10 where index is always an integer; positive for numbers greater than 1 and negative for numbers less than 1.

When writing out the full number on a place value diagram:

- A positive value of n gives the number of places that A moves to the left.
- A negative value of n gives the number of places that A moves to the right.

For example:

45,000 J = 4.5×10^4 J

0.000,052 m = 5.2×10^{-5} m

Energy 13

Comparing power

Question
Crane A lifts a load of 500 kg through a distance of 50 m in 20 s. Crane B lifts a load of 500 kg through a distance of 150 m in 20 s. Compare the powers of the two cranes.

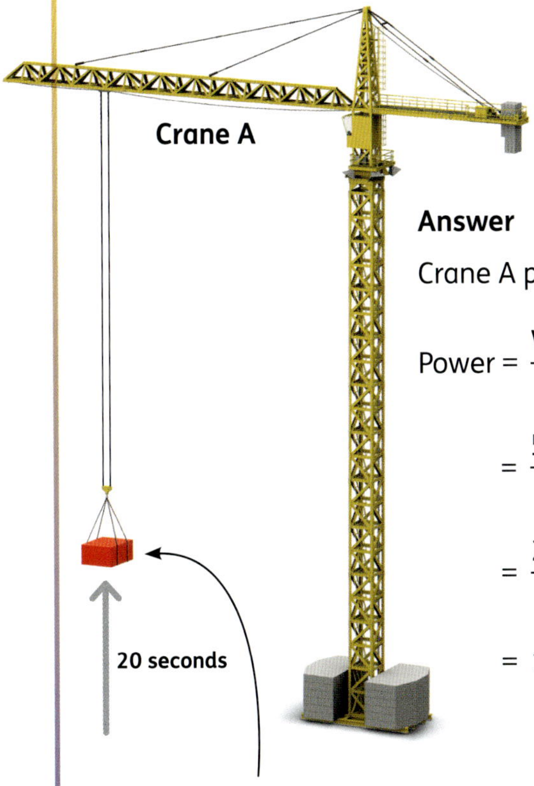

Crane A

Crane B

Answer
Crane A power:

$$\text{Power} = \frac{\text{Work done}}{\text{Time}}$$

$$= \frac{500 \times 50}{20}$$

$$= \frac{25{,}000}{20}$$

$$= 1{,}250 \text{ J}$$

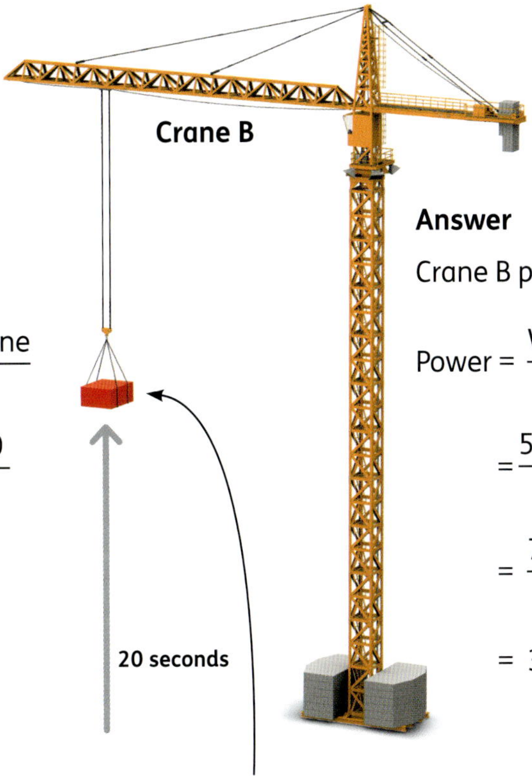

Answer
Crane B power:

$$\text{Power} = \frac{\text{Work done}}{\text{Time}}$$

$$= \frac{500 \times 150}{20}$$

$$= \frac{75{,}000}{20}$$

$$= 3{,}750 \text{ J}$$

20 seconds

20 seconds

The load lifted by each crane is the same, so the amount of energy required to lift them by the same height is the same.

This crane lifts the same load three times the height of the other crane in the same time. The power of its motor is three times that of the yellow crane.

How much power does a rocket need?

Rockets need engines that provide up to 60 gigawatts (60 billion watts) of power to escape the pull of Earth's gravity.

Energy Transfers in a System

Key facts

- The law of conservation of energy states that energy cannot be created or destroyed, but it can be transferred between stores.
- When energy is transferred, some energy is dissipated, or stored in less useful ways.
- Efficiency (%) = $\dfrac{\text{Useful output energy transfer}}{\text{Total input energy transfer}} \times 100\%$
- Efficiency (%) = $\dfrac{\text{Useful power output}}{\text{Total power input}} \times 100\%$

Reducing unwanted energy transfers

Most energy transfers in houses happen through the roof and walls. Energy is also transferred through windows, doors, and the ground. The rate of energy transfer is related to the difference in temperature between the outside and inside of the house. The greater the difference in temperature, the greater the rate of energy transfer.

In houses, unwanted energy transfers are reduced by using thicker materials and materials with a lower thermal conductivity. The lower the thermal conductivity of a material, the lower the rate of energy transfer by conduction across the material.

Wasted energy

When the light bulb (shown below) transfers energy, some of the energy is transferred to stores that are less useful – it is wasted or dissipated. In this case, it is the energy transferred to the thermal store of the surroundings that is wasted.

Calculating efficiency

Question
Calculate the efficiency of the LED bulb in the diagram.

Answer
Efficiency = $\dfrac{\text{Useful output energy transfer}}{\text{Total input energy transfer}}$

$= \dfrac{7}{10} \times 100\%$

$= 70\%$

Question
A fan transfers 5,000 J of energy. Of this, 300 J is transferred to thermal energy stores, 800 J is transferred through sound waves. The rest is transferred to useful kinetic energy stores. Calculate the efficiency of the fan.

Answer
Efficiency = $\dfrac{\text{Useful output energy transfer}}{\text{Total input energy transfer}} \times 100\%$

$= \dfrac{5{,}000 - 300 - 800}{5{,}000} \times 100\%$

$= \dfrac{3{,}900}{5{,}000} \times 100\%$

$= 78\%$

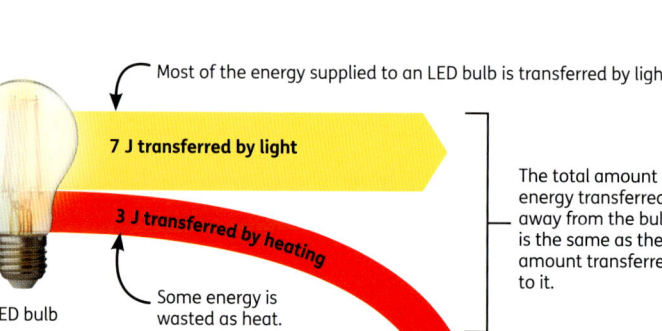

LED bulb — 10 J transferred by electricity; 7 J transferred by light; 3 J transferred by heating. Most of the energy supplied to an LED bulb is transferred by light. Some energy is wasted as heat. The total amount of energy transferred away from the bulb is the same as the amount transferred to it.

Energy 15

Methods of reducing unwanted energy transfers in a house include:

- Adding insulation in the roof and under the floor.
- Masonry blocks with trapped air.
- Thicker walls
- Double or triple glazed windows.
- Curtains over the windows and carpets on the floor.
- Tight fitting doors and windows to reduce draughts.

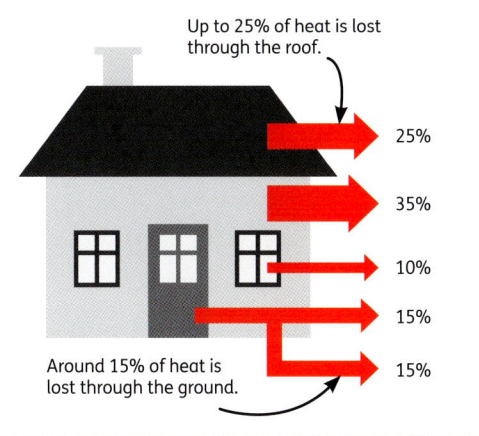

Up to 25% of heat is lost through the roof.

25%
35%
10%
15%
15%

Around 15% of heat is lost through the ground.

Science skills

Investigating insulation
Use this equipment to find out which material is the best insulator.

- Record the temperature every minute for at least 10 minutes.
- Measure the temperature drop with no insulation, as a control.
- Plot a graph of temperature against time for all three beakers on the same axes.
- The best insulator is the material that shows the smallest temperature drop over the 10 minutes.

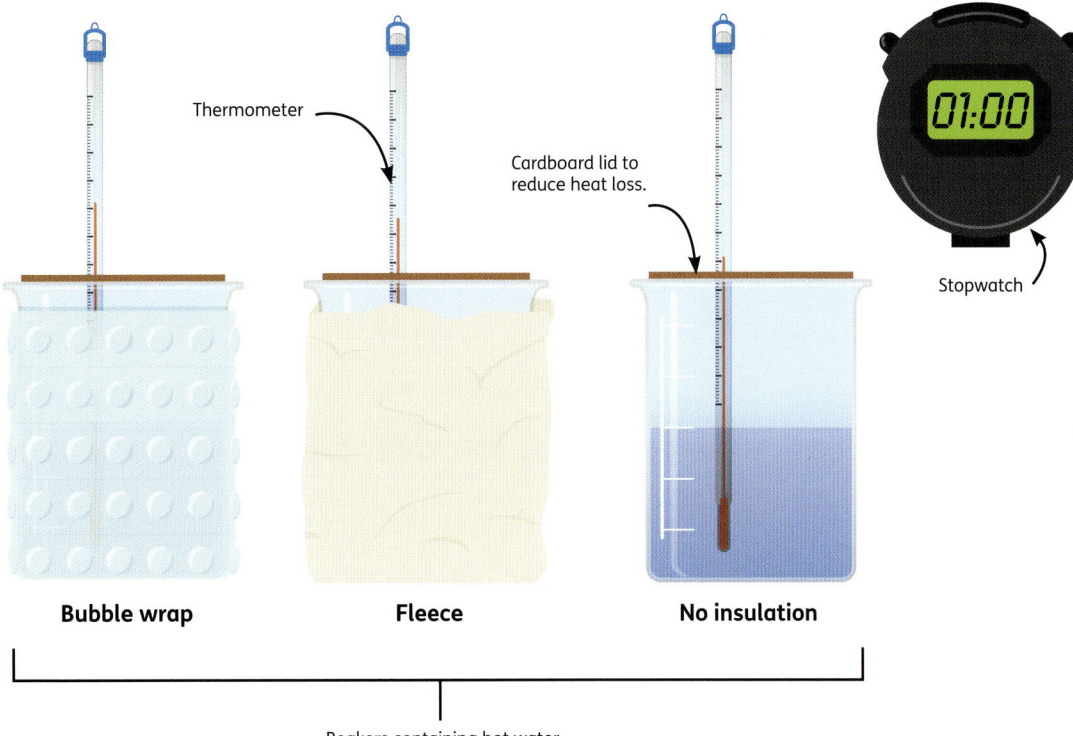

Thermometer

Cardboard lid to reduce heat loss.

Stopwatch

Bubble wrap **Fleece** **No insulation**

Beakers containing hot water

National and Global Energy Resources

Key terms

- **Non-renewable energy resources** cannot be replenished and will eventually run out.
- **Renewable energy resources** can be replenished as they are being used.

Uses of energy resources

Energy resources are used for transport, to generate electricity and to heat homes and other buildings.

- Fossil fuels and electricity are used for transport, heating and to make products.
- Fossil fuels and all renewables are used to generate electricity.

Energy resources

Energy resources can be renewable or non-renewable.

Non-renewable resources are fossil fuels such as coal and natural gas. They harm the environment and so many countries are trying to increase their use of renewable resources such as wind, hydroelectric, solar and tidal power.

The graph shows how the use of different energy resources has changed over time.

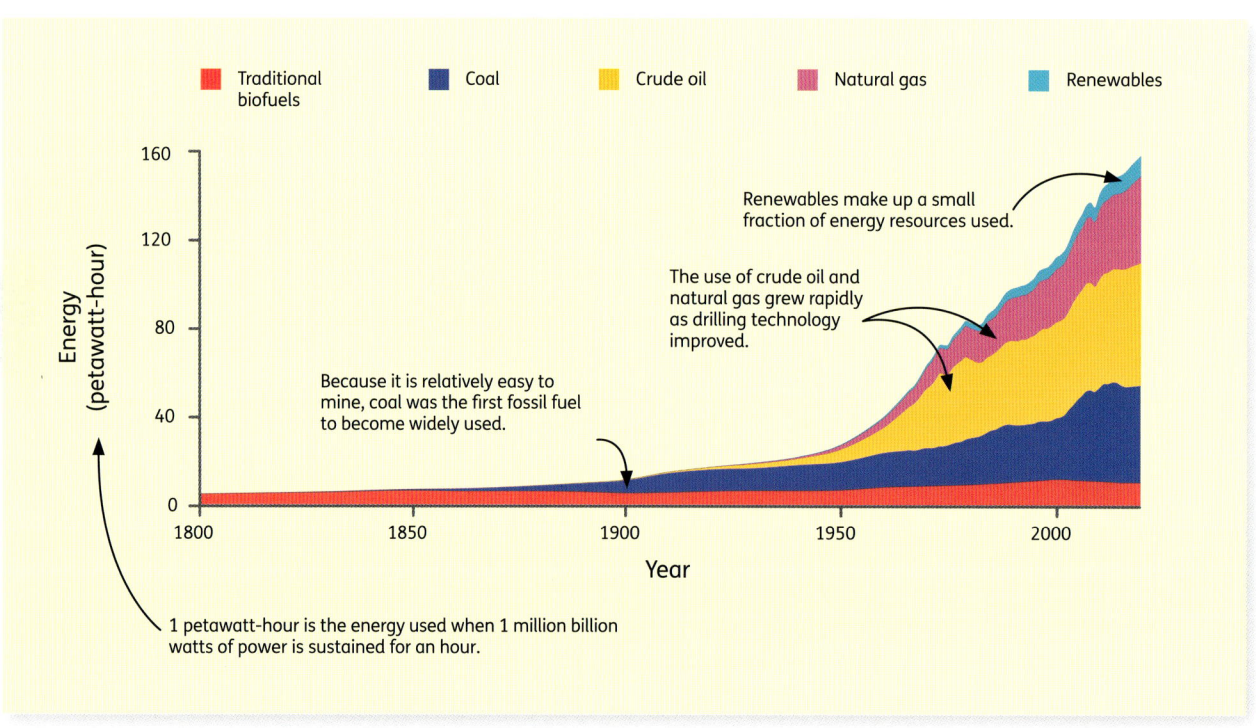

Reliability of energy resources

Some energy resources are more reliable than others.

- Fossil fuels are reliable because they are readily available and easy to use. We can use them when we need them.
- Solar, wind and hydroelectricity all rely on weather conditions, which are not predictable.
- On days with little sunshine and no wind, very little electricity can be generated from solar and wind.
- If there are long periods with little or no rain, hydroelectricity cannot generate very much electricity.
- The times of the tides are very predictable, but these times may not coincide with peak demand for electricity.

Carbon capture

Carbon capture is a technology that could be used to reduce emissions of carbon dioxide when fossil fuels are burned at power stations. The carbon dioxide is mixed with chemicals called amines to form a liquid. This liquid is then stored underground. Carbon capture could reduce emissions from power stations by 90 per cent. However, the electricity produced would be more expensive.

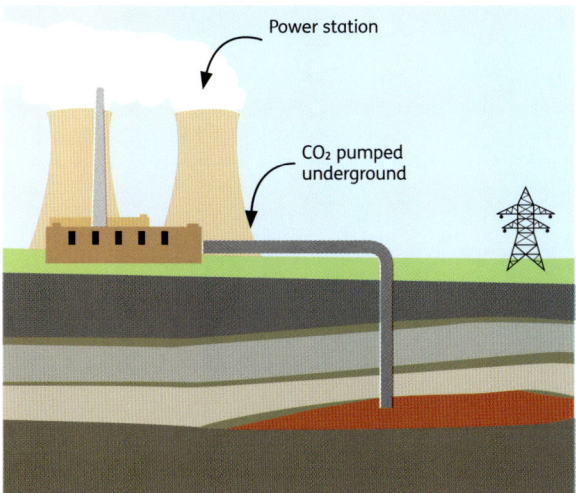

Environmental issues

Nuclear power produces radioactive waste, which will be dangerous for many thousands of years. Nuclear power plants are also very expensive to build.

When fossil fuels are burned they produce carbon dioxide, which contributes to global warming.

Some people do not like to see wind turbines and large numbers of solar panels in natural landscapes.

Reservoirs for hydroelectric power stations can flood land.

RAPPING UP!

Coal, oil and natural gas –
Fossil fuels, we burn, en masse.
At the power plant, quick as a flash,
Energy is sent to us for our cash.

Non-renewable **energy** from below.
We've used it for many years now so it's low.
Pollutes the air, CO_2 and CO.
But there are other types out here that I'll show.

Sun, wind, water. That's three.
Tides, **hydroelectricity**.
That's five. Now let me finish in full.
Last two, bio and geothermal.

They're renewable, so they'll never run out.
But they don't produce the greatest amount.
Plus they're **unreliable**.
But they're undeniable.

(Now) before I finish this song,
I'm gonna explain my favourite one:
Hydroelectric power is strong.
Uses **gravitational energy** from water.

That's up high by this dam.
Travels through a **turbine**
shaped like a fan.
Generates power
when it is span.
You can call them ugly,
I don't give a damn.

18 Brain Booster

Energy Recap Quiz

 Find a pen and paper and work through these revision questions.

1. A lamp is connected to a battery. Describe the energy transfers that take place between stores.

2. Define the law of conservation of energy.

3. A book of mass 0.75 kg is moved from the floor to a shelf 2 m above the floor. Calculate the change in the book's gravitational potential energy.
The gravitational field strength is 9.8 N/kg.

4. An unstretched spring has a length of 15 cm. It is stretched to a length of 20 cm. The spring constant of the spring is 250 N/m.
Calculate the elastic potential energy stored in the spring.

5. A train has a mass of 250,000 kg. It is moving at 30 m/s.
Calculate the kinetic energy of the train. Give your answer in standard form.

6. A TV transfers 2 J of energy by sound, 10 J of energy by light and 18 J of energy by heating every second.
   a) Which energy transfers are wanted?
   b) Which energy transfers are unwanted?
   c) Calculate the power of the TV.
   d) Calculate the efficiency of the TV.

7. How can you increase the efficiency of a device?

8. Define the term "renewable energy resource".

9. Give **two** examples of renewable energy resources.

Check your answers on page **109**.

Electricity

At the end of this chapter, you should be able to:

- ✓ Recognise and use circuit symbols in circuit diagrams.
- ✓ Recall and use the equation for charge and the equation linking potential difference, current and resistance.
- ✓ Explain how the resistance of different components changes depending on current through them and other conditions.
- ✓ Define the term "ohmic conductor".
- ✓ Explain the differences between series and parallel circuits.
- ✓ Calculate resistance in a series circuit.
- ✓ Explain the difference between alternating current and direct current.
- ✓ Explain the features of the mains electricity supply to an electrical device.
- ✓ Recall and use the equations for power in a circuit and energy transferred by everyday appliances.
- ✓ Explain how objects can become electrostatically charged.
- ✓ Explain what an electric field is.

Electricity

Circuits, Charge and Current

Key facts

- Electric circuits can be shown on a circuit diagram using recognised symbols for the components.
- An electric current is the flow of electric charge.
- A circuit needs a source of potential difference to push the charge around the circuit.

Exam tip

- In a closed circuit, a switch is closed so that it completes the circuit.
- In an open circuit, a switch is open so there is a gap in the circuit.

Circuit symbols

Components can be represented by circuit symbols.

switch (closed)	cell	battery	diode
resistor	variable resistor	light-emitting diode (LED)	light-dependent resistor (LDR)
lamp	fuse	thermistor	voltmeter
ammeter			

Electricity

Circuit diagrams

The symbols used for components are standard, which means anyone can interpret a circuit diagram. Connecting wires are represented by straight lines.

Circuit diagram

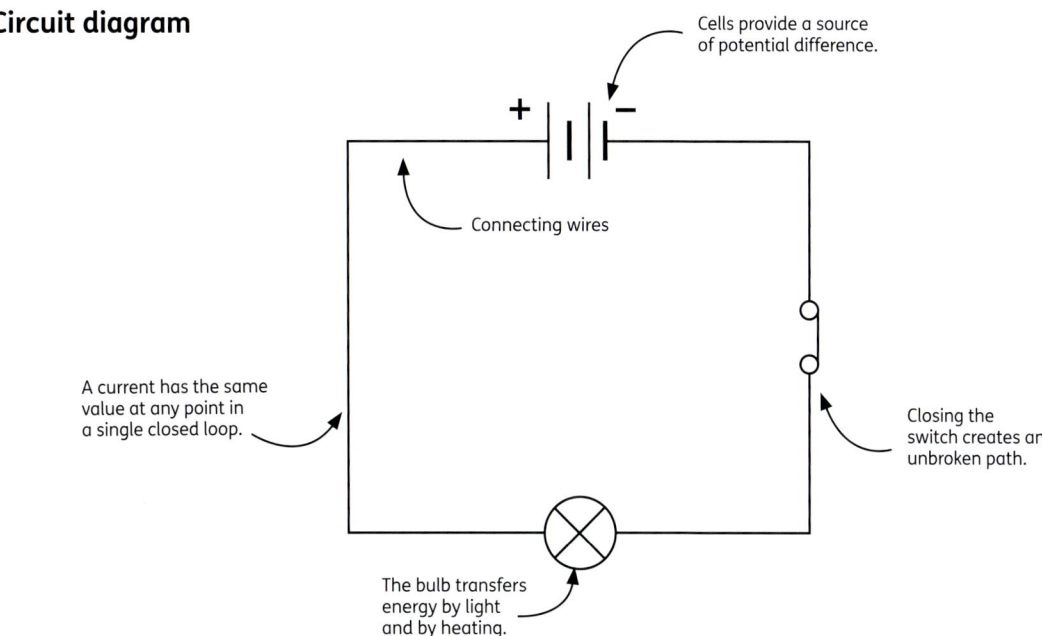

Charge and current

Charge is measured in **coulombs**.

Electric current is a flow of electrical charge. You can think of a current as being like water flowing through a pipe. The size of the electric current is the rate of flow of electrical charge. 1 amp is 1 coulomb per second.

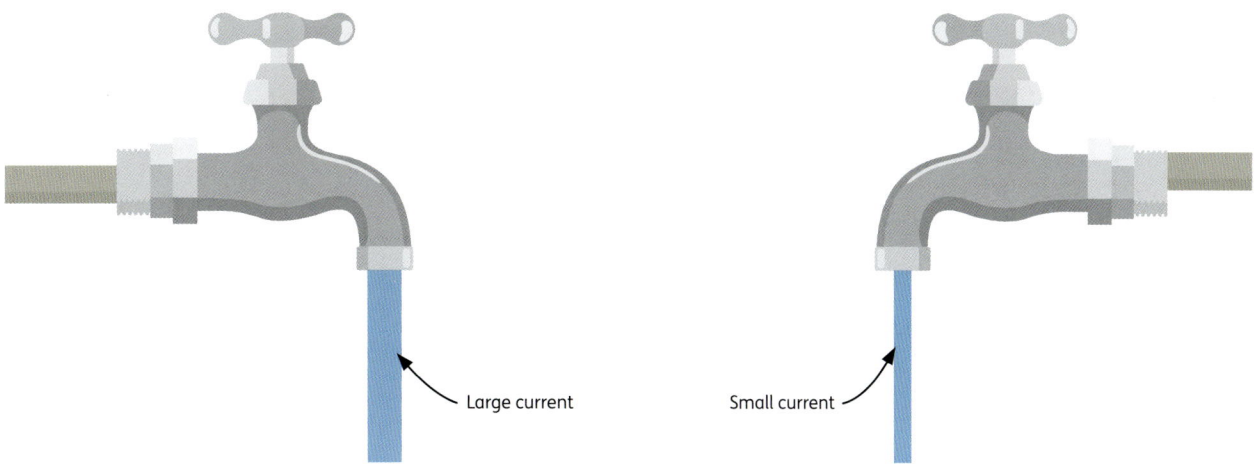

For electrical charge to flow through a circuit, there must not be any gaps in the circuit. It must be a closed circuit.

The circuit must include a source of potential difference, for example a cell.

Electricity

Current, Resistance and Potential Difference

Key facts

- Charge (in C) = Current (in A) × Time (in s)
- Potential difference (in V) = Current (in A) × Resistance (in Ω)
- The resistance of a wire is proportional to its length.

Calculating charge

Question
A digital radio is switched on for 5 minutes and a current of 0.25 A flows through it.

Calculate the charge that passes through the radio.

Answer
First convert time to seconds:

5 minutes = 5 × 60 = 300 seconds

Charge = Current × Time

= 0.25 × 300

= 75 C

Question
A tablet puts out a maximum current of 2.4 A. Calculate the charge that flows through it when the tablet is used for 10 minutes.

Answer
First convert the time to seconds:

10 minutes = 10 × 60 = 600 seconds

Charge = Current × Time

= 2.4 × 600

= 1,440 C

Here's how **electricity** works.
Let's start with the circuit first.
The electrons flow from the power source,
then through the wire they surge.

As they pass through components
energy gets transferred.
This bulb lights up in a moment.
To understand you need to know three words.

Now the first word's **voltage**.
It's always misunderstood.
It measures the PUSH of electrons.
Higher volts then greater the push.

The second word's **current**.
So I'm a tell you now and not later.
It measures the flow electrons.
Up the volts and watch the amps gets greater.

The third word's **resistance**.
It reduces electron flow.
If you increase resistance (**ohms**)
the lower the current will go

Now we can work out resistance.
We just put this one in front.
Resistance will then equal
the voltage divided by current.

Electricity

Calculating potential difference

Question
The current through a light bulb is 0.04 A. The resistance of the light bulb is 5.75 kΩ. Calculate the potential difference across the light bulb.

Answer
5.75 kΩ = 5,750 Ω

Potential difference = Current × Resistance
= 0.04 × 5,750
= 230 V

Question
A torch bulb has a current of 0.25 A and a resistance of 12 Ω. Calculate the potential difference.

Answer
Potential difference = Current × Resistance
= 0.25 × 12
= 3 V

Science skills

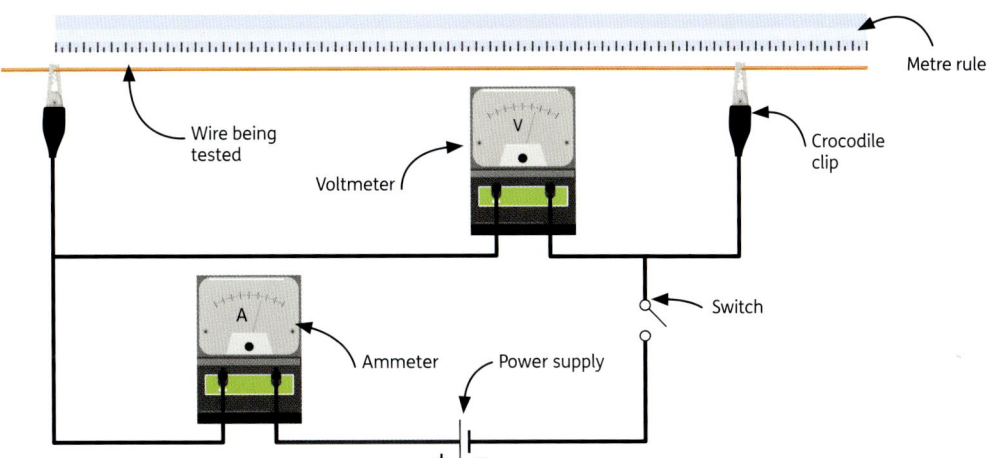

You can investigate how the resistance of a wire varies with length using the equipment shown in the diagram.

- Record the potential difference across and the current through the wire for different lengths of wire.
- Calculate the resistance of the wire using the equation

$$\text{Resistance} = \frac{\text{Potential difference}}{\text{Current}}$$

- Plot a graph of resistance (on the vertical axis) against length (on the horizontal axis).
- Draw a line of best fit through the points.
- If the line passes through the origin, this shows that resistance is directly proportional to length.

Possible sources of error

- Zero of metre rule not correctly aligned with the crocodile clip.
- Resistance from other wires in the circuit.

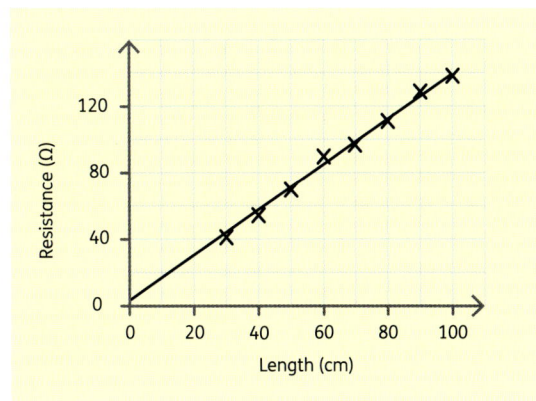

Electricity

Resistors

Key facts

- In an ohmic conductor, resistance remains constant.
- The resistance of components such as lamps, diodes, thermistors and LDRs is not constant; it changes with the current through the component.
- The resistance of a thermistor changes with temperature.
- The resistance of a light-dependent resistor changes with the intensity of light shining on it.

Ohmic conductors

When the temperature remains constant, the current through an ohmic conductor is directly proportional to the potential difference across the resistor. A graph of current against potential difference is a straight line that goes through the origin. The resistance remains constant as the current changes: $V = IR$.

A resistor is an ohmic conductor.

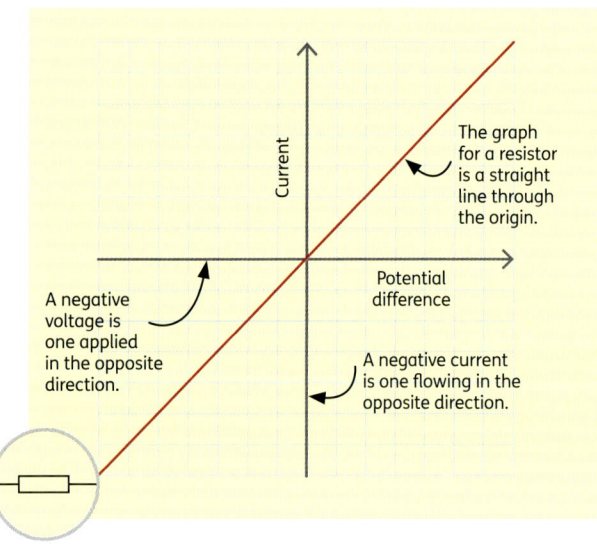

The graph for a resistor is a straight line through the origin.

A negative voltage is one applied in the opposite direction.

A negative current is one flowing in the opposite direction.

Resistance of other components

The resistance of filament lamps and diodes changes as the current through the component changes. A graph of current against potential difference is not a straight line.

Filament lamp

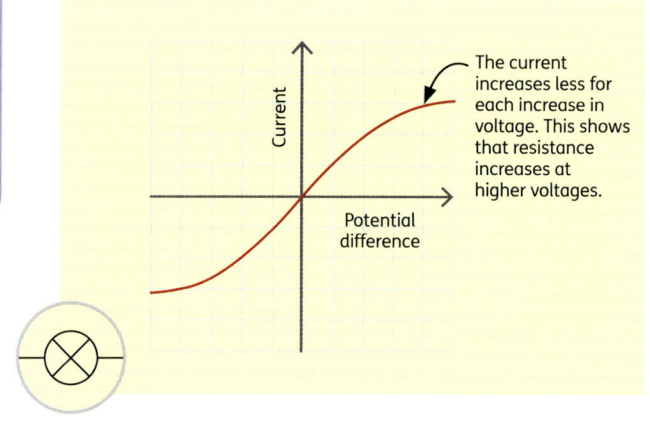

The current increases less for each increase in voltage. This shows that resistance increases at higher voltages.

Diode

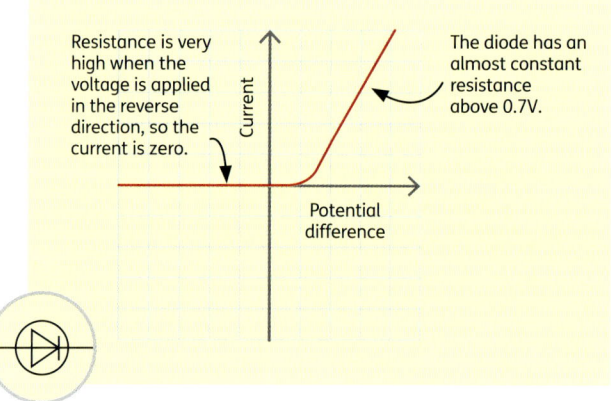

Resistance is very high when the voltage is applied in the reverse direction, so the current is zero.

The diode has an almost constant resistance above 0.7V.

Changing resistance

You can change the resistance in a circuit to control how much current can flow using a variable resistor. A variable resistor has a coil of resistance wire and a sliding contact. The sliding contact changes how much of the coil the current passes through. Variable resistors are used in circuits that control dimmer switches, the volume controls on electrical devices, or the speed of motors in washing machines.

Electricity

Light-dependent resistor (LDR)
The resistance of an LDR decreases as the intensity of light shining on it increases.

An LDR can be used in a circuit to switch lights on when it gets dark.

Thermistor
The resistance of a thermistor decreases as its temperature increases.

A thermistor can be used as a thermostat to switch a circuit on or off at a certain temperature. Using a variable resistor in the same circuit allows the temperature at which the circuit switches on or off to be changed.

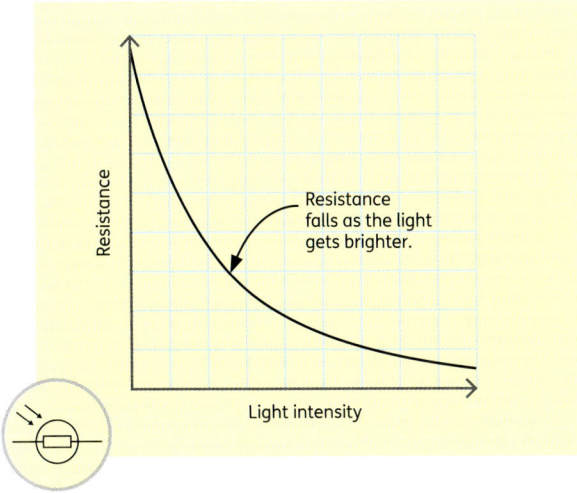

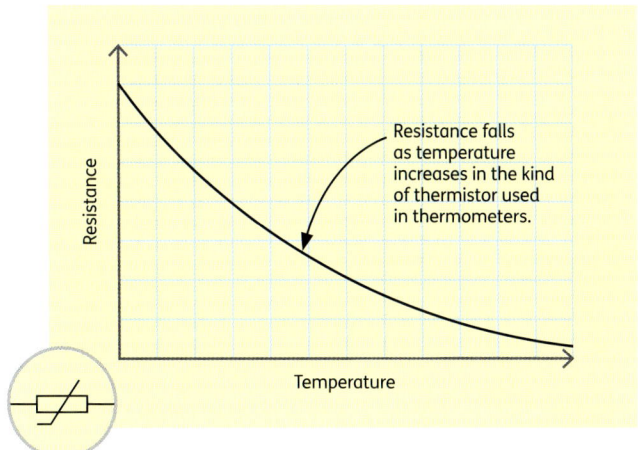

Science skills

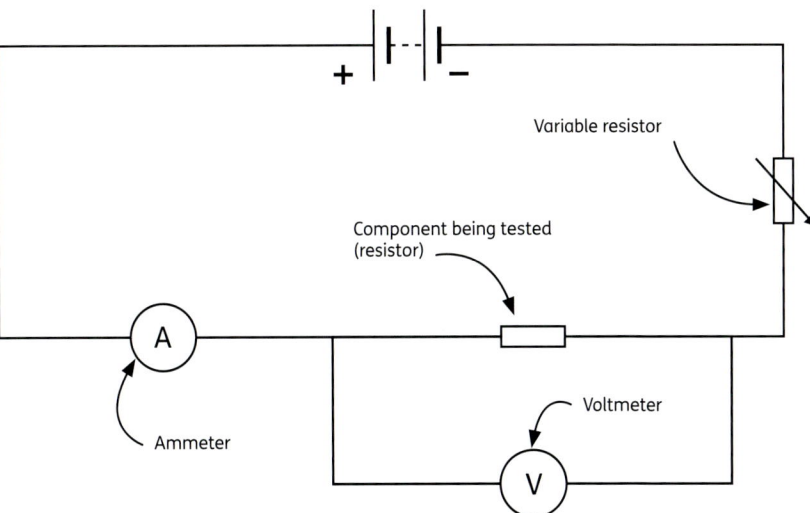

- You can investigate the resistance of a component using the circuit shown in the diagram.
- Replace the resistor with the component you are testing.
- Record the current for different values of potential difference.
- Use the equation Resistance = $\dfrac{\text{Potential difference}}{\text{Current}}$ to calculate resistance.

Electricity

Series and Parallel Circuits

Key facts

- Electrical circuits can be connected in series or parallel.
- In a series circuit there is one loop for the current to flow through.
- In a parallel circuit there is more than one branch for the current to flow through.

A series circuit connected in a single loop is used in a torch. The circuits that are used in houses for lighting are called parallel circuits. This is where the circuit splits into branches.

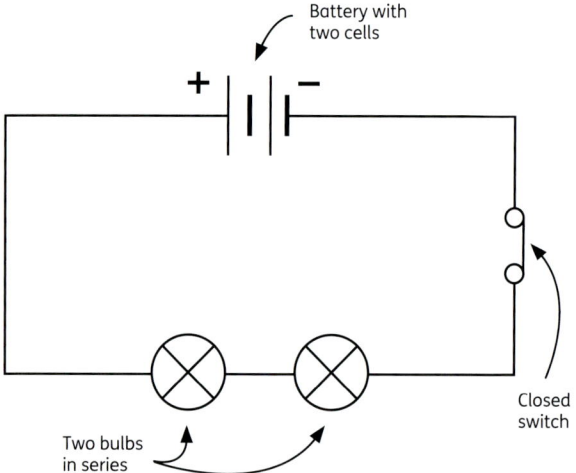

Battery with two cells
Two bulbs in series
Closed switch

Series circuits

In the circuit in the diagram, the bulbs are connected in series.

- There is one path that the current can flow through.
- If one bulb breaks, there is a gap in the circuit and no current can flow.
- The potential difference is shared between the two bulbs.

Parallel circuits

In the circuit in the diagram, the bulbs are connected in parallel.

- There are two paths that the current can flow through.
- If one bulb breaks, there is still a loop that the current can flow through so the circuit continues to work.
- The potential difference across each bulb is the same.

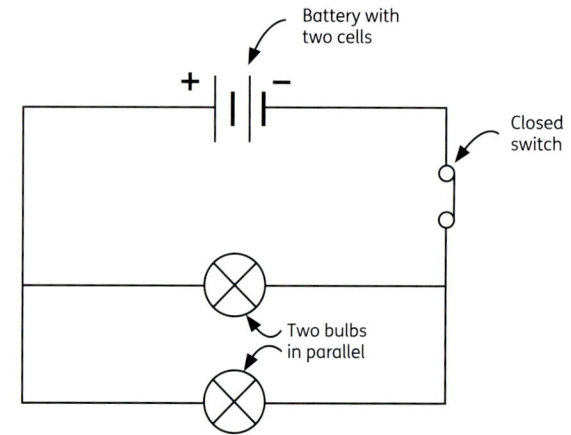

Battery with two cells
Closed switch
Two bulbs in parallel

RAPPING UP!

These are parallel and **series circuits**.
The difference? Here's how to interpret.
Series circuits, here's how it goes.
All components are lined up all in a row.

In parallel – there's some advances.
Components are on **multiple branches**.
For current and voltage - you need to know,
how this affects them, so let me show.

One **wire**, one **cell**, one **switch** and two **bulbs**.
The currents the same in each one as it flows.
But, parallels not the same.
Current is shared – like a second name
(Mr and Mrs Green).

Voltage in series is shared.
Parallel voltage it is not.
That's why when comparing the circuits,
parallel gets as bright as it got.

Electricity

Resistance

In the series circuit:

- The current has to flow through both bulbs and is the same through each bulb.
- The total resistance is the sum of the resistance of each bulb.

$R_{total} = R_1 + R_2$

In the parallel circuit:

- The current only has to flow through one bulb, so it is easier for the current to flow around the circuit.
- The total resistance is less than the resistance of either of the bulbs.

Question
a) Calculate the total resistance of the resistor and bulb.
b) Calculate the current flowing in the circuit.

Answer
a) $R_{total} = R_1 + R_2$
    $= 50\,\Omega + 100\,\Omega$
    $= 150\,\Omega$

b) Current $= \dfrac{\text{Potential difference}}{\text{Resistance}}$

    $= \dfrac{9}{150}$

    $= 0.06$ A or 60 mA

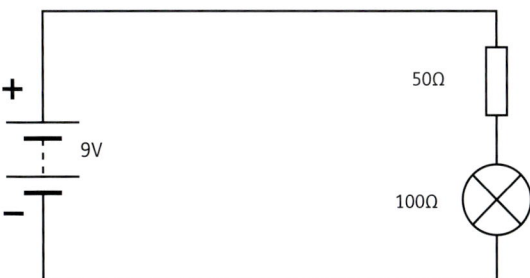

Science skills

Measuring current and potential difference

- When you are measuring the current through a component, you connect an ammeter in series with the component.
- When you are measuring the potential difference across a component, you connect a voltmeter in parallel with the component.

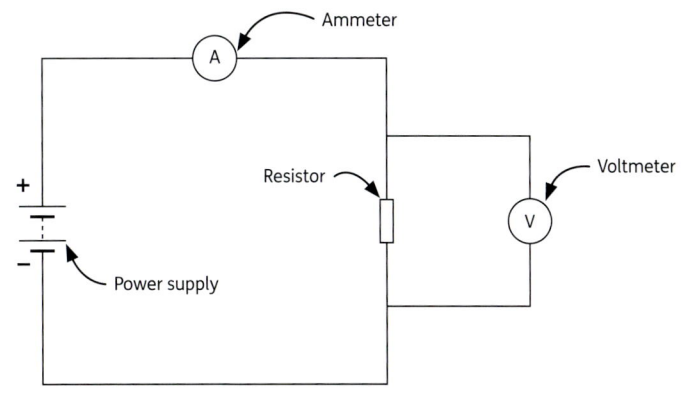

Electricity

Domestic Uses and Safety

Key facts

- In direct current, the current flows in one direction but in alternating current it is constantly changing direction.
- The mains supply is an alternating current (ac) supply, at 230 V and 50 Hz.
- The wires that connect appliances to plugs have two or three wires in them.
- The wires are colour-coded and each has a different function.

UK mains supply

In the UK, the domestic electricity supply is an alternating current (ac) supply with a frequency of 50 Hz and a potential difference of about 230 V.

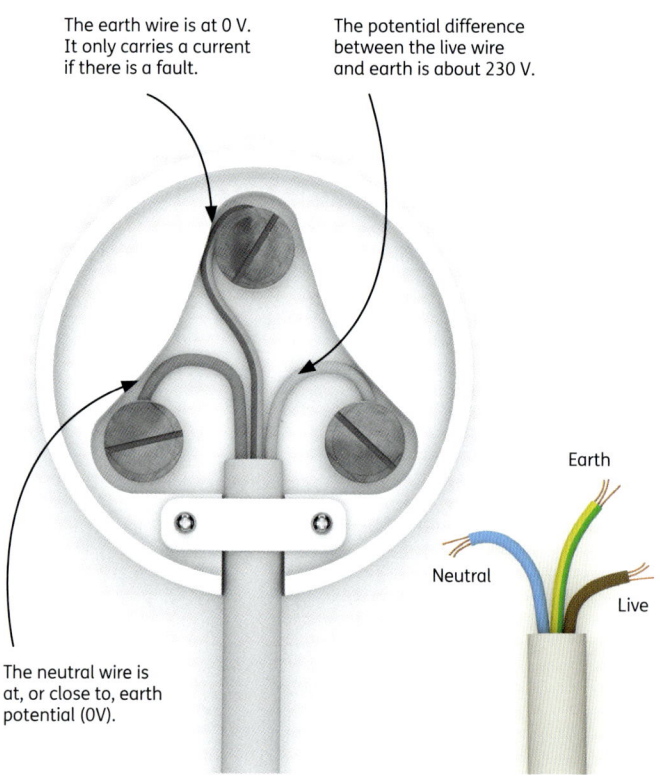

The earth wire is at 0 V. It only carries a current if there is a fault.

The potential difference between the live wire and earth is about 230 V.

The neutral wire is at, or close to, earth potential (0V).

Earth / Neutral / Live

Electrical safety

The earth wire is a safety wire that stops an appliance becoming live.

A live wire may be dangerous even when a switch in the mains circuit is open because, if you touch it, your body can complete the circuit to Earth. You would then get an electric shock.

The live wire is always connected to a fuse or circuit breaker.

When there is a fault, the current is cut off by the fuse melting or the circuit breaker tripping.

Faulty and not earthed

The person's body completes the circuit by providing a route for electricity to reach the ground.

Ground / Large current / A faulty wire allows electricity to flow through the washing machine case.

Faulty but earthed

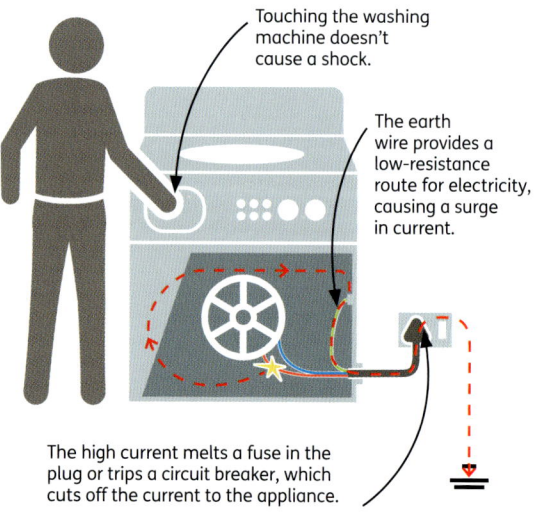

Touching the washing machine doesn't cause a shock.

The earth wire provides a low-resistance route for electricity, causing a surge in current.

The high current melts a fuse in the plug or trips a circuit breaker, which cuts off the current to the appliance.

Electricity

Direct current (dc)

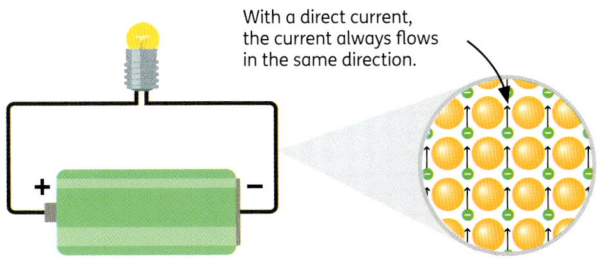

With a direct current, the current always flows in the same direction.

Alternating current (ac)

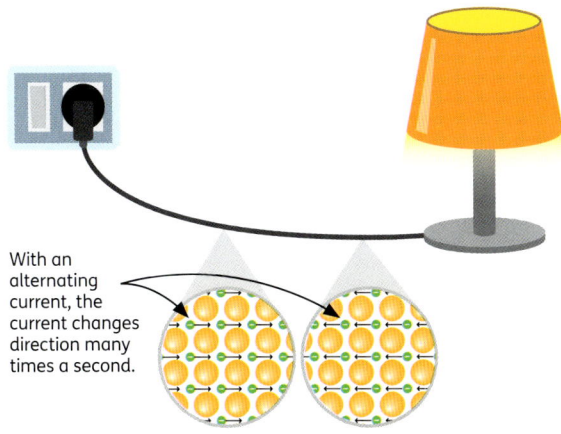

With an alternating current, the current changes direction many times a second.

Converting alternating current to direct current

To convert alternating current to direct current, a rectifier is used. A rectifier is made up of diodes, which only allow current to flow in one direction.

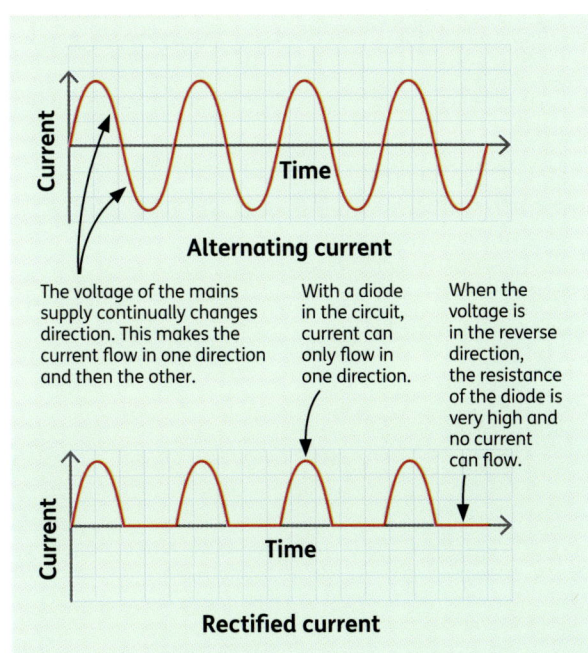

The voltage of the mains supply continually changes direction. This makes the current flow in one direction and then the other.

With a diode in the circuit, current can only flow in one direction.

When the voltage is in the reverse direction, the resistance of the diode is very high and no current can flow.

RAPPING UP!

To understand plugs, this is required.
This one is the fuse and these three are the wires.
Brown is called live, touching it is dire.
Carries a current straight through to this drier.

This wire returns it, blue's its attire.
We call it **neutral** in case you enquire.
The last one is **earth** – its purpose inspires.
Prevents you from shock and meeting someone higher.

If there is damage, the earth will acquire
the extra current and make sure it retires.
Green and yellow is the colour. Now it transpires.
And here is the **fuse**, without it there's fire.

Think you can't pass? You still got time yet.
There are two currents – the first one's direct.
Second alternating – I can dissect.
Just look at the screen – it's coming on my left.

DC is direct, current's one direction.
Not the comic or the band – sorry if distressing.
You find this type in **batteries** – I won't keep you guessing.
Here are some examples – ain't no need for stressing.

AC alternating – it just goes back and forth.
You find this in the mains - you cannot ignore.
Feeling like a **compass**, there's southside and the north.
Let's call this a day for now we won't do any more.

Electricity

Energy Transfers

> ### Key facts
>
> - Power (in W) = Potential difference (in V) × Current (in A)
> - Power (in W) = (Current (in A))² × Resistance (in Ω)
> - Energy transferred (in J) = Power (in W) × Time (in s)
> - Energy transferred (in J) = Charge flow (in C) × Potential difference (in V)
> - Transformers are used to increase the voltage for long distance transmission to reduce energy losses in the cables.

What is power?

Power is a measure of the rate at which energy is transferred. A higher power means more energy is transferred per second.

The food blender transfers 10 times as much energy per second as the immersion heater. It transfers about one-third of the energy transferred per second by the hairdryer.

Calculating power

Question
The current through a food blender is 2.2 A. It is connected to a mains supply of 230 V.

Calculate the power of the food blender.

Answer
Power = Potential difference × Current

= 230 × 2.2

= 506 W

Question
The resistance of an immersion heater used in the laboratory is 3 Ω. The current flowing through the immersion heater is 4 A.

Calculate the power of the immersion heater.

Answer
Power = (Current)² × Resistance

= 4² × 3

= 16 × 3

= 48 W

Question
Calculate the power of a bulb when the current through it is 0.5 A and the potential difference across it is 6 V.

Answer
Power = Potential difference × Current

= 6 × 0.5

= 3 W

Electricity

Calculating energy transferred

Question
The power of a hairdryer is 1,500 W. Calculate the energy transferred when the hairdryer is used for 5 minutes.

Answer
Convert time to seconds:

5 minutes = 5 × 60 = 300 seconds

Energy transferred = Power × Time

$\qquad$ = 1,500 × 300

$\qquad$ = 450,000 J (or 450 kJ or 4.5×10^5 J)

The hairdryer transfers energy to the thermal and kinetic energy stores of the air. It also transfers energy to the thermal energy store of parts of the hairdryer.

Question
The potential difference across a fan is 3 V.
The charge flow through the fan is 40 C.
Calculate the energy transferred by the fan.

Answer
Energy transferred = Charge flow × Potential difference

$\qquad$ = 40 × 3

$\qquad$ = 120 J

The National Grid

Electrical power is transferred from power stations to consumers by a network of cables and transformers. This network is called the National Grid.

All cables have resistance, even though it is small. Power loss in the cables is equal to (current)² × resistance. Increasing the voltage (potential difference) reduces the current in the wires. If the current is halved, the power loss decreases by a factor of 4, as power loss is proportional to current squared.

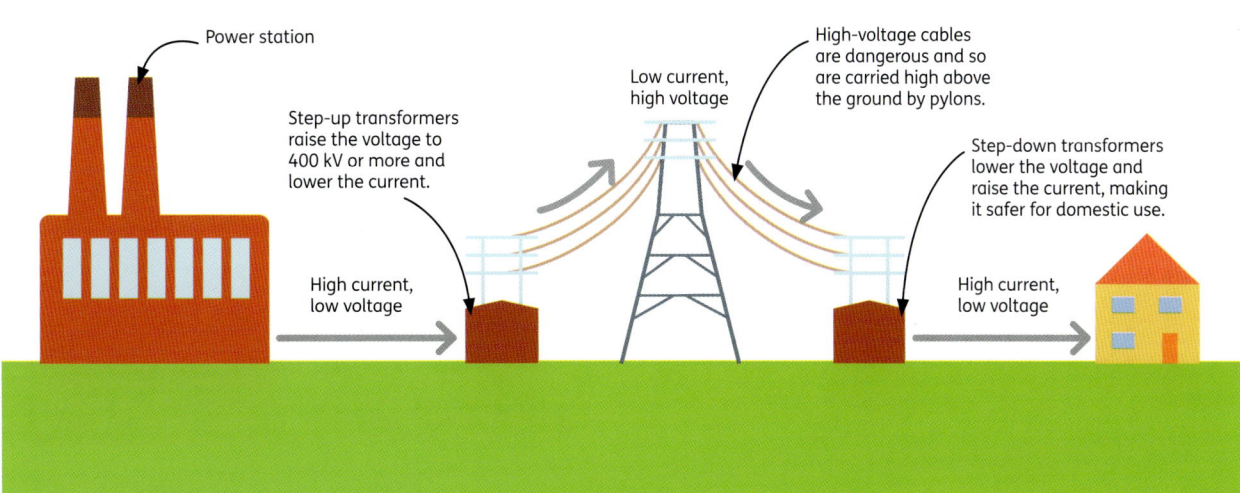

Power station

Step-up transformers raise the voltage to 400 kV or more and lower the current.

High current, low voltage

Low current, high voltage

High-voltage cables are dangerous and so are carried high above the ground by pylons.

Step-down transformers lower the voltage and raise the current, making it safer for domestic use.

High current, low voltage

Electricity

Static Electricity

Static charge

When some insulators are rubbed together, electrons are transferred from one material to the other.

The material that loses electrons becomes positively charged and the material that gains electrons becomes negatively charged.

When two electrically charged objects are brought close together, they exert a non-contact force on each other. If the charges are both positive or both negative, the objects repel each other. If the charges are opposite, the objects attract each other.

Key facts

- When you rub some insulators together, they can become charged with static electricity.
- When two electrically charged objects are brought close together they exert a force on each other.
- A charged object creates an electric field around itself.

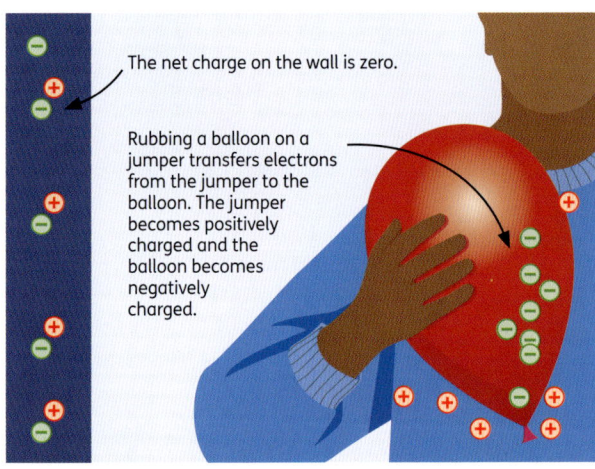

The net charge on the wall is zero.

Rubbing a balloon on a jumper transfers electrons from the jumper to the balloon. The jumper becomes positively charged and the balloon becomes negatively charged.

When the balloon is near the wall, the negative charge on the balloon repels electrons in the wall. The surface of the wall near the balloon becomes positively charged.

The opposite charges attract each other and the balloon sticks to the wall.

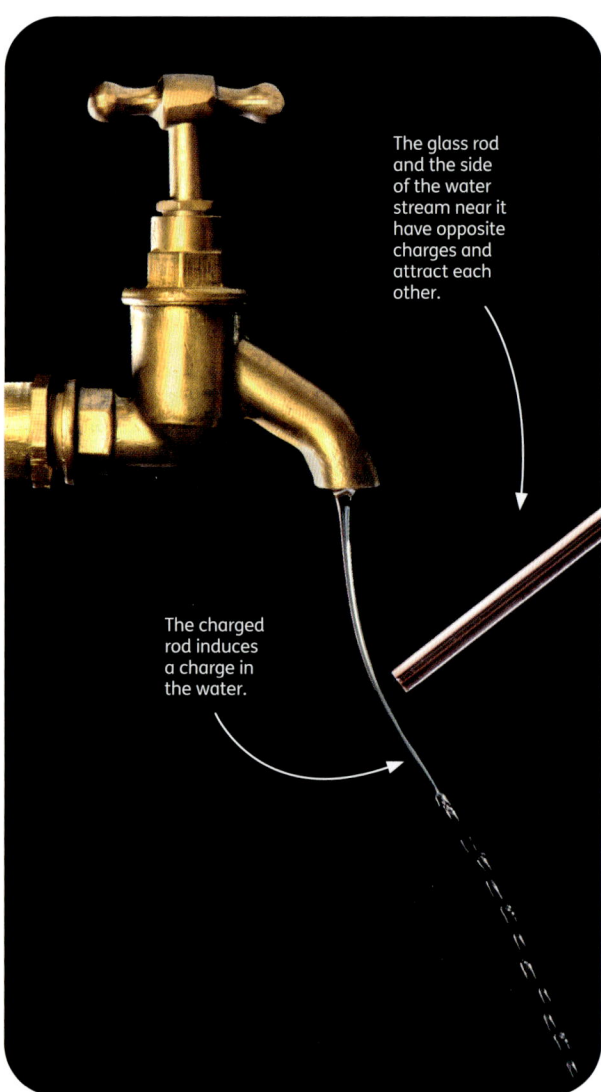

The glass rod and the side of the water stream near it have opposite charges and attract each other.

The charged rod induces a charge in the water.

Electricity

Dangers of static electricity

Lightning
Static electricity can build up inside a thundercloud when water droplets and ice pass each other quickly. A lightning bolt is a giant spark of static electricity which is only a few centimetres wide but its length is measured in kilometres. The transfer of electrical energy heats the air around it to around 30,000°C, which produces the brilliant light. The sudden release of thermal energy makes the air expand. This produces the sound of thunder. Lightning can strike a person directly or start fires if it strikes buildings. This is why tall buildings often have a lightning conductor which will direct the charge directly to Earth if the building is struck.

Refuelling aircraft
A spark of static electricity could start a fire during refuelling of aircraft. Charge could build up between the fuel truck and the aircraft as a result of friction from the rapid movement of large volumes of fuel. This is why, when an aircraft is being refuelled, wires connect the aircraft to the fuel truck. The wires stop charge building up between the truck and the aircraft.

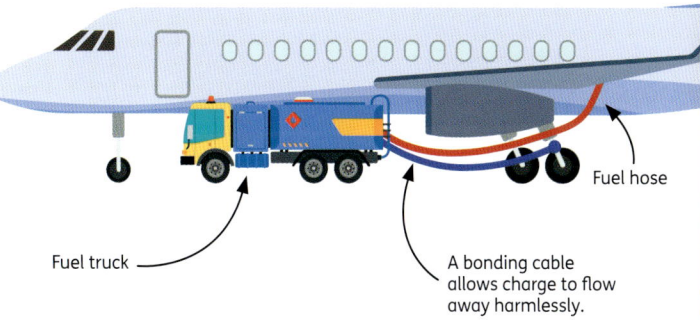

Fuel hose
Fuel truck
A bonding cable allows charge to flow away harmlessly.

Electric fields

A charged object creates an electric field around itself that is strongest close to the charged object. The further away from the charged object, the weaker the field.

When another charged object is placed in the electric field of the first object, both objects experience a force. The force increases as the objects get closer together.

Field around a positive charge

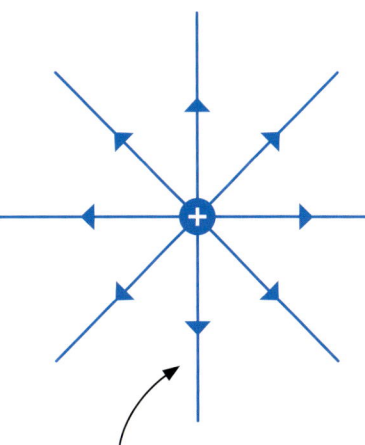

Arrows show the direction of the force on positive charges.

Field around a negative charge

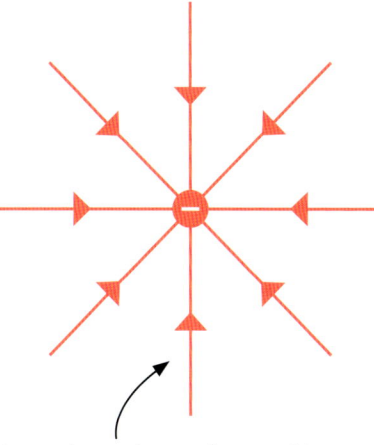

Arrows always point away from a positive charge and towards a negative charge.

Parallel plates

The electric field between two parallel plates that have opposite charges has the same strength everywhere between the plates except near the ends.

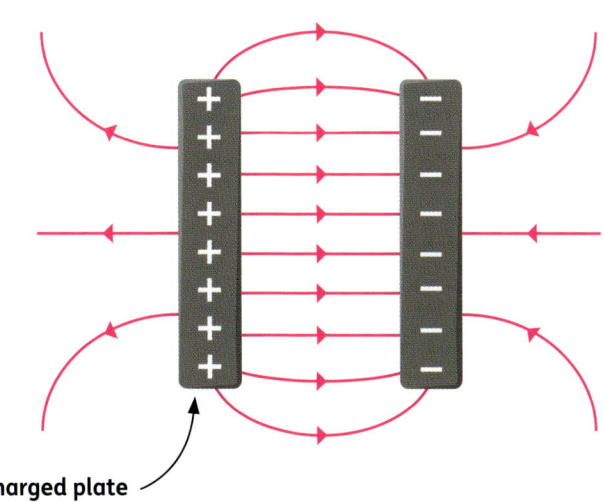

Charged plate

Brain Booster

Electricity Recap Quiz

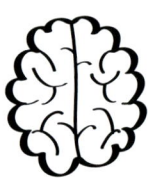

 Find a pen and paper and work through these revision questions.

1. a) Draw a circuit diagram with two cells, a switch and a bulb connected in series.
   b) Add an ammeter to measure the current through the bulb and a voltmeter to measure the potential difference across the bulb.

2. Draw the circuit symbols for a thermistor and an LED.

3. Draw a circuit diagram for the investigation shown on page 23.

4. The power rating of a laptop is 40 W. Calculate how much energy is transferred when the laptop is switched on for 2 hours.

5. Give the colours of the earth, live and neutral wires in a UK plug.

6. Explain how the earth wire helps to protect you from an electric shock.

7. a) The current through a light bulb is 0.05 A. It is switched on for 30 minutes. Calculate the charge flow through the light bulb.
   b) The light bulb is connected to a mains supply of 230 V. Calculate the amount of energy transferred by the light bulb.

8. Describe how transformers are used in the UK National Grid.

9. Explain how an insulator can become charged.

10. Draw an electric field pattern for a small positively charged sphere.

Check your answers on page **109**.

Particle Model of Matter

At the end of this chapter, you should be able to:

- ✓ Recognise and draw diagrams to show the differences between solids, liquids and gases.
- ✓ Calculate density.
- ✓ Determine the density of liquids and regular and irregular shaped objects.
- ✓ Describe how mass is conserved when a substance changes state.
- ✓ Explain that internal energy is the total of the kinetic energy and potential energy of the particles.
- ✓ Calculate specific heat capacity and energy changes during changes of state.
- ✓ Define the term "specific latent heat".
- ✓ Explain how the motion of the molecules in a gas is related to both its temperature and its pressure.
- ✓ Explain the relation between the temperature of a gas and its pressure at constant volume.
- ✓ Calculate the change in the pressure of a gas or the volume of a gas.

Density and States of Matter

Key facts

- In solids, particles are close together in fixed arrangements.
- In liquids, particles are close together but can move around.
- In gases, particles are a long way apart and can move around.
- Density (in kg/m³) = $\dfrac{\text{Mass (in kg)}}{\text{Volume (in m}^3\text{)}}$

Particles in a solid

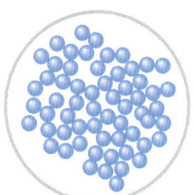

Particles in a liquid

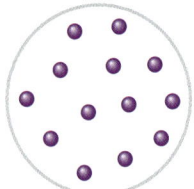

Particles in a gas

The temperature of a substance is related to the energy of the particles in the substance. Particles in solids have lower energy than particles in liquids, and particles in liquids have lower energy than particles in gases. This graph shows have the termperature of a block of ice changes over time when you heat it.

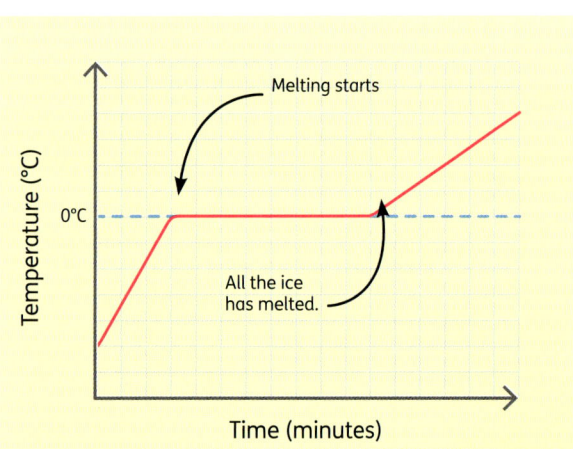

RAPPING UP!

I'm gonna teach you **states of matter** while tryna be the greatest rapper. There's solid, liquid and gas. All three states are made up of mass.

All three states are made up of **atoms**. You'll hear things you can't even fathom. **Solids** first: I'll show you their pattern. Have fixed shapes; I'll show how it happens.

They're arranged in layers, in rows. They **vibrate** but bet they can't flow. Call it strange, their energy's low. With heat exchange they start to move slow.

Now it's **liquids**, here I can show. As heat's absorbed, the energy grows. They still touch, although not in rows. Now atoms slide **above and below**.

We're not done now, there's more to know. With more energy atoms can go away from each other, no longer touching. Move so **quickly**, and it's like they're rushing.

That's the last thing I'm going to serve. What's taking place in this heating curve. It's right here that the **temperature rises**. But at this place here it is preserved.

Particle Model of Matter   37

Density and particles

Why does a brick have a mass that is far greater than a sponge of the same volume?

The brick weighs more because it has a greater mass.

The sponge has less mass but a similar volume – it's less dense.

The brick has fewer air spaces than the sponge. It is more dense than the sponge.

Calculating density

Question
A 20 cm cube of copper has a mass of 71.68 kg. Calculate the density of copper.

Answer
20 cm = 0.2 m

Volume of cube = $(0.2)^3$ = 0.008 m^3

Density = $\dfrac{\text{Mass}}{\text{Volume}}$

= $\dfrac{71.68}{0.008}$

= 8,960 kg/m^3

Science skills

To determine the density of a liquid:
- Use a balance to find the mass of a measuring cylinder.
- Add a known volume of liquid to the measuring cylinder and find its mass.
- Subtract the mass of the empty cylinder from the mass of the cylinder and liquid.

To determine the density of an object:
- Use a balance to find the mass of the object.
- For a regularly shaped object, measure its dimensions then work out the volume.
- For an irregularly shaped object, use the displacement method to work out the volume.

In all cases, use the density equation to calculate the density.

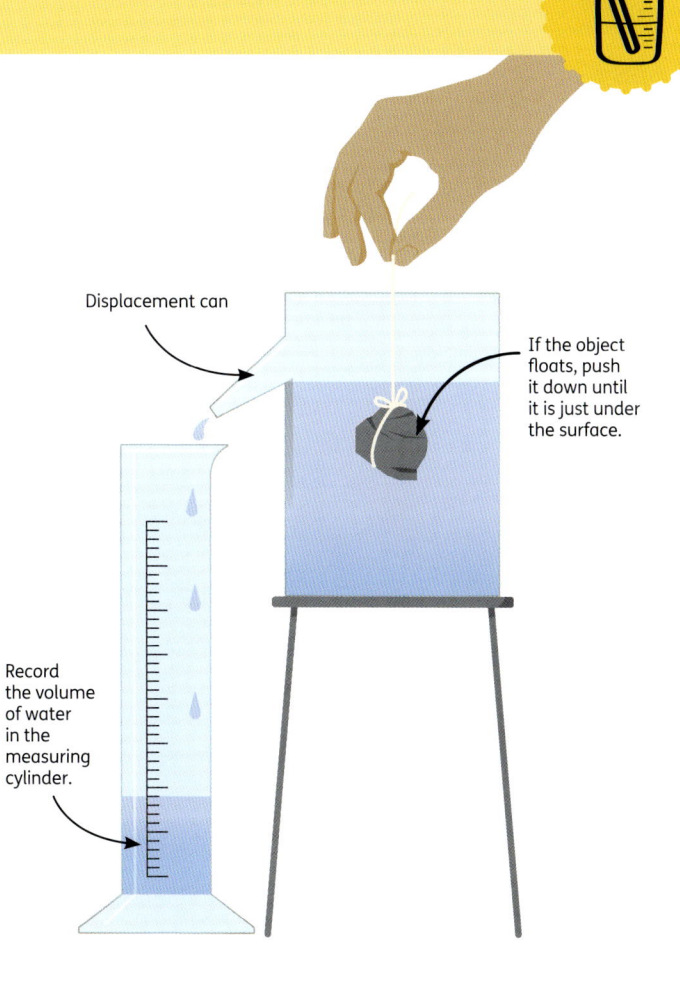

Displacement can

If the object floats, push it down until it is just under the surface.

Record the volume of water in the measuring cylinder.

Changes of State and Internal Energy

Key facts

- Mass is conserved when an object changes state.
- Internal energy is the total of the kinetic energy and potential energy of the particles.

Changes of state

Changes of state are physical changes because the change can be reversed and the material recovers its original properties. No new substances are produced in a physical change.

When an ice cube melts, the number of water molecules does not change. So the mass of the water is the same as the mass of the ice cube – mass is conserved. This is true for all changes of state.

Changing state

Water can exist in three different states: ice, water and gas (steam or water vapour). Clouds and the mist that forms above boiling kettles are made of tiny drops of water.

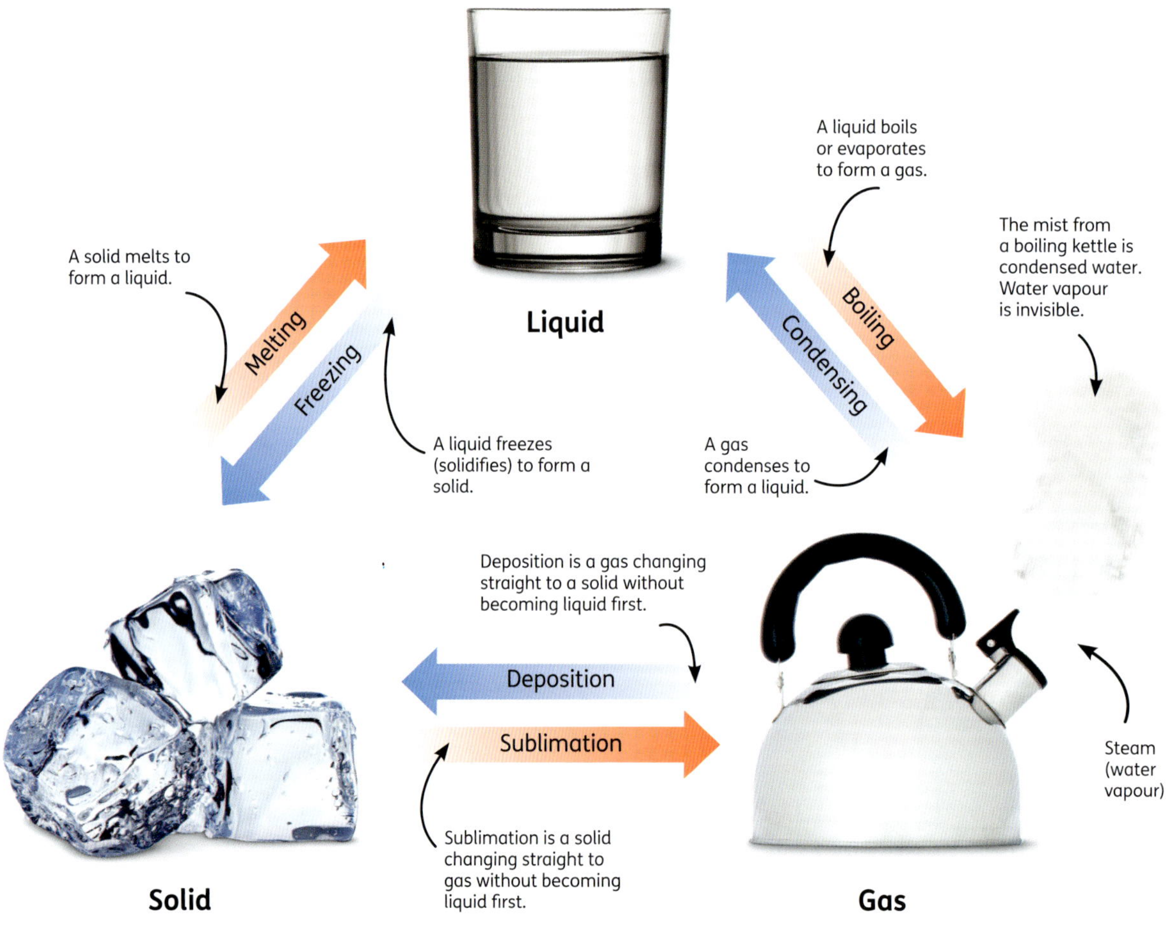

Liquid

A solid melts to form a liquid.

A liquid boils or evaporates to form a gas.

The mist from a boiling kettle is condensed water. Water vapour is invisible.

Melting / Freezing

Boiling / Condensing

A liquid freezes (solidifies) to form a solid.

A gas condenses to form a liquid.

Deposition is a gas changing straight to a solid without becoming liquid first.

Deposition

Sublimation

Sublimation is a solid changing straight to gas without becoming liquid first.

Solid

Gas

Steam (water vapour)

Particle Model of Matter

Internal energy

The particles (atoms and molecules) that make up a system store energy, which is known as internal energy. Particles in solids vibrate backwards and forwards, and the particles in liquids and gases move about randomly.

Internal energy is the total kinetic energy and potential energy of all the particles in a system.

When you heat a solid, liquid or gas, the kinetic energy of the particles increases. This increases the temperature of the object.

Temperature is a measure of the average kinetic energy of the particles but it is not a measure of the internal energy of the object.

Heating can also change the state of the object. When an object changes state, energy is transferred to the object to break the bonds between the particles so that they can move more freely. The potential energy of the particles increases, but the kinetic energy of the particles remains the same.

Exam tip

Internal energy is to do with the energy of the particles. It is not to do with the object that the particles are in. Internal kinetic energy is not the kinetic energy of the object. Internal potential energy is not the gravitational potential energy of the object.

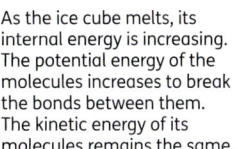

As the ice cube melts, its internal energy is increasing. The potential energy of the molecules increases to break the bonds between them. The kinetic energy of its molecules remains the same.

An iceberg has a much greater store of internal energy than a cup of hot coffee because it has more particles.

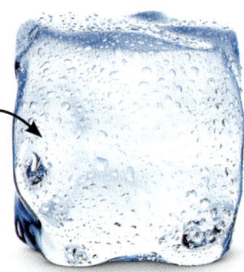

The water particles in a hot drink are moving faster than in ice, giving it a higher temperature. But a cup of coffee has less internal energy than an iceberg because it has fewer particles.

Particle Model of Matter

Energy Transfers

> ### Key facts
> - The specific latent heat of a substance is the amount of energy required to change the state of one kilogram of the substance with no change in temperature.
> - Change in thermal energy (in J) = Mass (in kg) × Specific heat capacity (in J/kg °C) × Temperature change (in °C)
> - Energy for a change of state (in J) = Mass (in kg) × Specific latent heat (in J/kg)

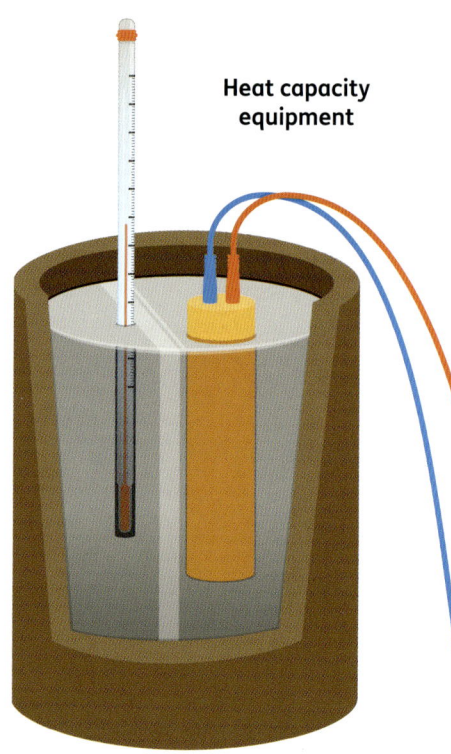

Heat capacity equipment

Calculating specific heat capacity

The specific heat capacity of a substance is the amount of energy required to raise the temperature of 1 kilogram of the substance by 1 degree Celsius.

Question
A student carries out an investigation to find the specific heat capacity of copper. The student heats a block of copper of mass 0.8 kg. The starting temperature is 20°C and the final temperature is 60°C. The amount of energy transferred to the block is 12.32 kJ.

Calculate the specific heat capacity of copper.

Answer
Specific heat capacity =
$$\frac{\text{Change in thermal energy}}{\text{Mass} \times \text{Temperature change}}$$

Temperature change = 60 − 20 = 40°C

Specific heat capacity = $\frac{12{,}320}{0.8 \times 40}$ = 385 J/kg°C

Question
A student carries out an investigation to find the specific heat capacity of aluminium.

The student heats a block of aluminium of mass 1 kg. The starting temperature is 18°C and the final temperature is 42°C. The amount of energy transferred to the block is 22,313 J.

Calculate the specific heat capacity of aluminium.

Answer
Temperature change = 42 − 18
= 24°C

Specific heat capacity =
$$\frac{\text{Change in thermal energy}}{\text{Mass} \times \text{Temperature change}}$$
$$= \frac{(22{,}313)}{(1 \times 24)}$$
= 929.7 J/kg°C

Particle Model of Matter

Specific latent heat

Latent heat is the energy needed to melt a substance or to evaporate it.

When a substance is melting, boiling, condensing or freezing, its temperature does not change.

The amount of energy required to change the state of one kilogram of the substance with no change in temperature is the specific latent heat.

The amount of energy needed to change state from solid to liquid is the specific latent heat of fusion.

The amount of energy needed to change state from liquid to vapour is the specific latent heat of vaporisation.

More energy is needed to separate particles completely to turn a liquid into a gas than is needed to break the bonds in a solid and turn it into a liquid. So the latent heat of vaporisation is much higher than the latent heat of fusion.

Question
There is 500 g of water in the beaker in the photo. Calculate how much energy is needed to evaporate the water.

The specific latent heat of vaporisation of water is 2,256,000 J/kg.

Answer
Convert mass to kg: 500 g = 0.5 kg

Energy for a change of state = Mass × Specific latent heat

= 0.5 × 2,256,000

= 1,128,000 J (or 1.128 MJ or 1.128×10^6 J)

Bubbles of water vapour

Heating and cooling curves

The graph shows how temperature changes with time as a substance changes state.

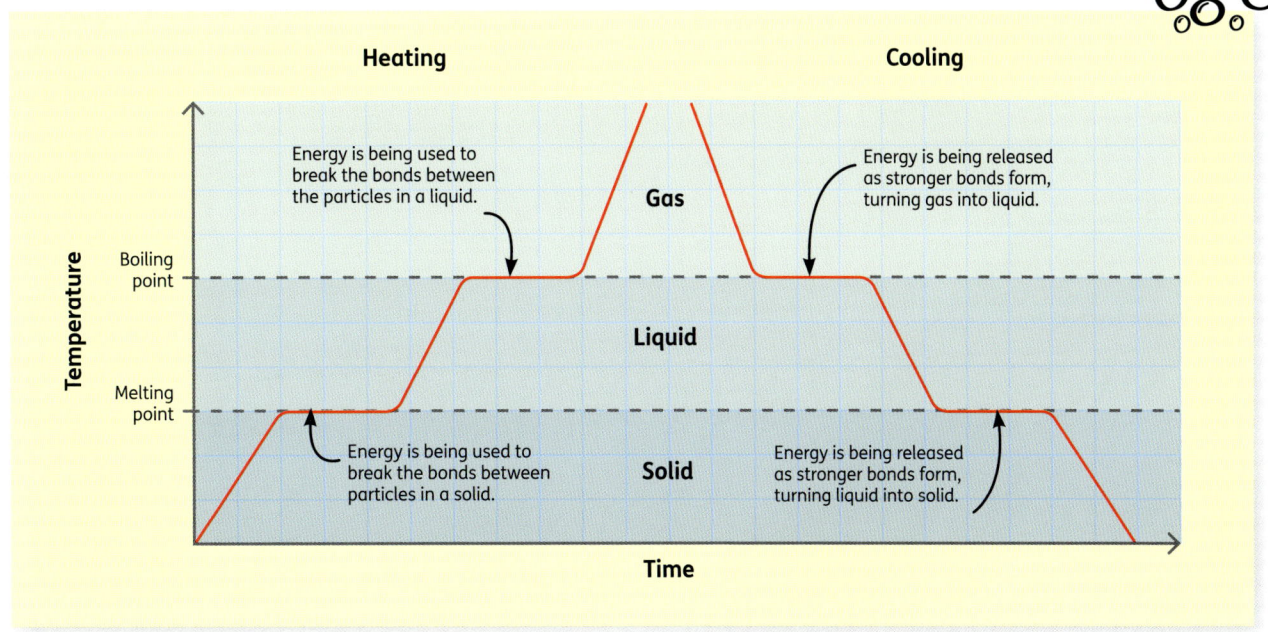

Particle Model and Pressure

Key facts

- Pressure produces a net force at right angles to the wall of the gas container.
- Heating a gas at constant volume increases its pressure. Cooling it reduces its pressure.
- The pressure of a gas at constant temperature is inversely proportional to volume.
- For a fixed mass of gas held at a constant temperature:
  Pressure (in Pa) × Volume = Constant

Particle model

The molecules of a gas are constantly moving in random directions. In a container, the gas particles collide with the walls of the container constantly. Each collision exerts a force that creates pressure.

Pressure and volume

Pressure and volume are inversely proportional, as long as the temperature does not change.

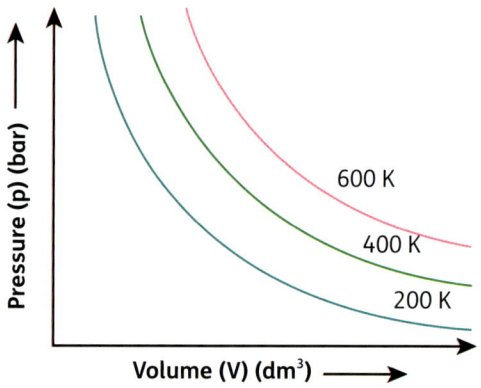

This means that when you multiply them together, the product remains the same:

$P_1 \times V_1 = P_2 \times V_2$

Reducing the volume of the gas increases the pressure. Increasing the volume of the gas reduces the pressure.

Gas particles are in constant random motion.

As a particle strikes the wall, it exerts a force.

As pressure inside rises, the tyre feels firmer.

Collisions are spread over a larger area, resulting in lower pressure.

Collisions are concentrated in a smaller area, resulting in higher pressure.

Particle Model of Matter

Pressure and temperature

When the temperature of the gas increases, the average kinetic energy of the molecules increases. The speed of the particles increases and they collide with the walls of the container harder and more often, which increases the pressure.

The particles collide with the container walls harder and more often, exerting more pressure.

The particles have more kinetic energy and move faster.

Low temperature | High temperature

Absolute zero

Temperature is a measure of the average kinetic energy of the particles in a substance. A higher temperature means that the particles in a substance are moving faster than they do at a lower temperature. There is a theoretical temperature at which all the particles in a substance are stationary. This temperature is called absolute zero. It is the starting point for the Kelvin temperature scale. A rise of 1 K is the same as a rise of 1°C.

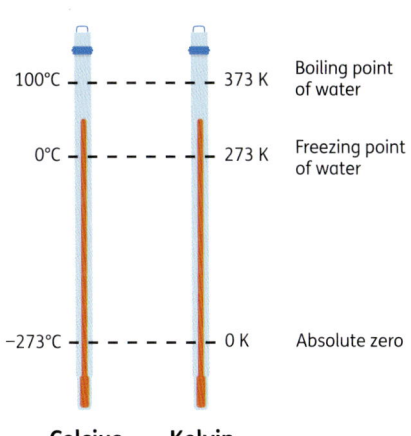

100°C — 373 K Boiling point of water
0°C — 273 K Freezing point of water
−273°C — 0 K Absolute zero

Celsius Kelvin

Calculating pressure and volume

Question
A container holds 0.5 m³ of air at a pressure of 100,000 Pa. The volume of the container is reduced to 0.2 m³. Calculate the new pressure, assuming that the temperature remains the same.

Answer
Pressure × Volume before = Pressure × Volume after

100,000 × 0.5 = Pressure after × 0.2

$$\text{Pressure after} = \frac{100,000 \times 0.5}{0.2}$$

$$= 250,000 \text{ Pa (or 250k Pa or } 2.5 \times 10^5 \text{ Pa)}$$

Kelvin scale

The Kelvin temperature scale measures temperature relative to absolute zero.

To convert to K from °C, add 273.

To convert to °C from K, subtract 273.

Particle Model of Matter
Recap Quiz

 Find a pen and paper and work through these revision questions.

1. In which state of matter are the particles close together and free to move?
2. Describe how to determine the density of a liquid.
3. A wooden door has dimensions 2 m by 5 cm by 75 cm and has a mass of 60 kg. Calculate the density of the door.
4. Define the term "internal energy".
5. Explain what happens to the internal energy of an object when the temperature increases.
6. Explain the difference between specific heat capacity and specific latent heat.
7. a) 2.5 kg of ice is taken from a freezer at −18°C and heated to 0°C. The energy transferred to the ice is 94,950 J. Calculate the specific heat capacity of the ice.
   b) Calculate the energy needed to melt the ice. The latent heat of fusion of water is 334,000 J/kg.
8. Explain how air molecules exert pressure in a container.
9. A container holds 1.5 m³ of air at a pressure of 150,000 Pa. The volume of the container is reduced and the new pressure is 450,000 Pa. Calculate the new volume, assuming that the temperature remains the same.

Check your answers on page **109**.

Atomic Structure

At the end of this chapter, you should be able to:

- ✓ Describe the structure and size of an atom.
- ✓ Represent atoms in symbol form.
- ✓ Explain what an isotope is.
- ✓ Describe the development of models of the atom.
- ✓ Explain the significance of the alpha particle scattering experiment.
- ✓ Describe the different types of nuclear radiation and their penetrating powers.
- ✓ Balance nuclear equations.
- ✓ Define half-life of a radioactive isotope.
- ✓ Explain the difference between contamination and irradiation.
- ✓ Describe the sources of background radiation.
- ✓ Describe hazards and uses of nuclear radiation.
- ✓ Describe nuclear fission and nuclear fusion.

Models of the Atom

> **Key facts**
> - The scientific model of the atom has changed over time because of new experimental evidence.
> - The alpha particle scattering experiment showed that most of the mass of an atom is in the nucleus.

Early model

The models we use to represent atoms have evolved as new experimental evidence has appeared. Atoms were originally thought to be tiny spheres that could not be divided any further.

Plum pudding model

The British physicist, J J Thomson, discovered the electron in 1897. This discovery led to the plum pudding model of the atom. In this model, the atom is a ball of positive charge (the pudding) with negative electrons embedded in it (the plums).

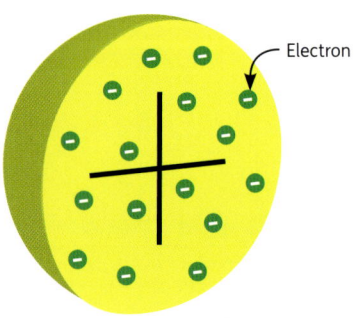

Rutherford model

In the early 1900s, a team of physicists led by Ernest Rutherford carried out experiments to study what happened when alpha particles passed through different substances, such as gold foil.

Most of the alpha particles passed straight through but a few were scattered. The plum pudding model could not explain this.

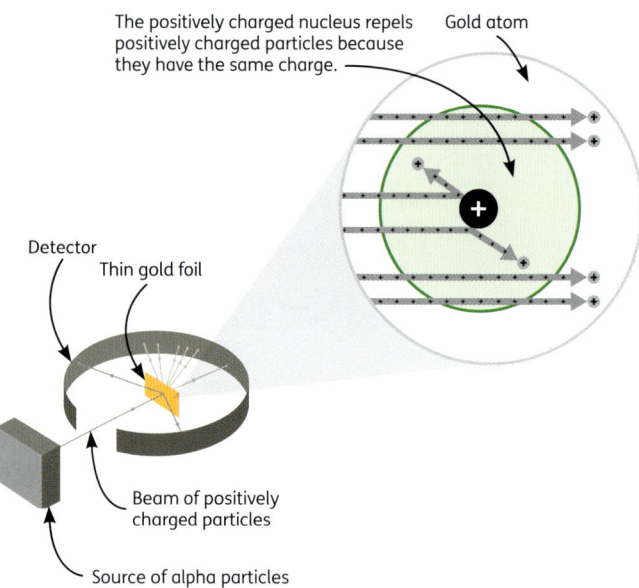

The conclusion of the alpha particle scattering experiment was that most of the atom was empty space, with most of the mass in a small positively charged nucleus.

Rutherford's model replaced the plum pudding model.

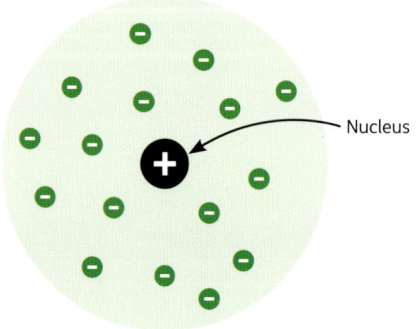

Atomic Structure

Bohr model

The physicist Niels Bohr suggested that electrons orbit the nucleus in specific energy levels at certain distances from the nucleus. This helped to explain why atoms emit or absorb only specific wavelengths of light.

The theoretical calculations of Bohr agreed with experimental observations.

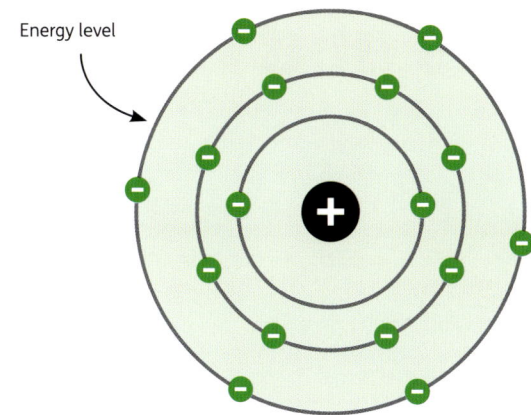

Protons and neutrons

Later experiments led to the discovery of the proton. The positive charge of any nucleus can be subdivided into a whole number of smaller particles. Each particle has the same amount of positive charge.

The physicist James Chadwick carried out experiments that provided the evidence to show the existence of neutrons within the nucleus. This happened about 20 years after the concept of the nucleus was accepted.

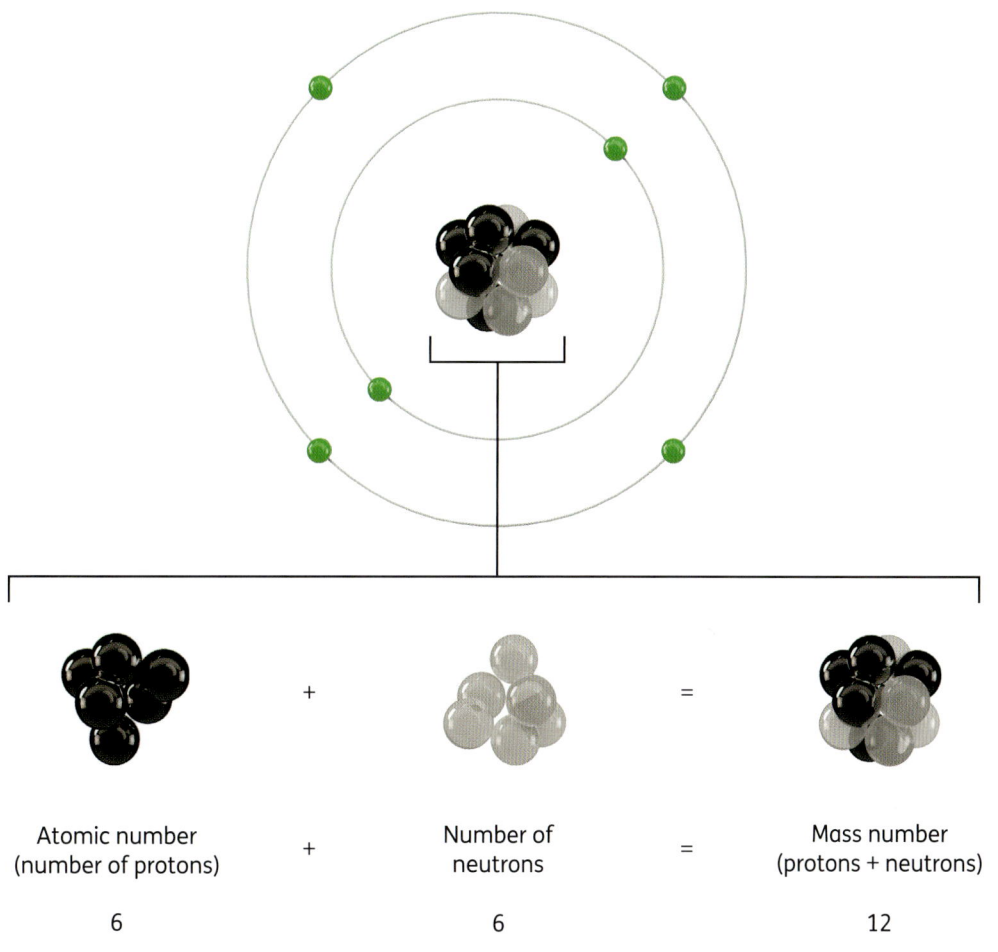

Atomic number (number of protons) + Number of neutrons = Mass number (protons + neutrons)

6 + 6 = 12

Atomic Structure

Atoms and Isotopes

Key facts

- Atoms are made up of protons, neutrons and electrons.
- The atomic number is the number of protons.
- The mass number is the number of protons and neutrons
- Isotopes are different forms of an element with different numbers of neutrons.

Structure of an atom

An atom has a nucleus containing protons and neutrons and contains most of the mass of the atom.

Electrons orbit the nucleus at different energy levels. When electrons move between energy levels, they do so by absorbing or emitting electromagnetic radiation. Low energy levels are closest to the nucleus and the energy increases with distance from the nucleus.

Particle	Charge	Mass	Location
Proton	+1	1	Inside nucleus
Neutron	0	1	Inside nucleus
Electron	−1	0.000,5	Orbiting the nucleus

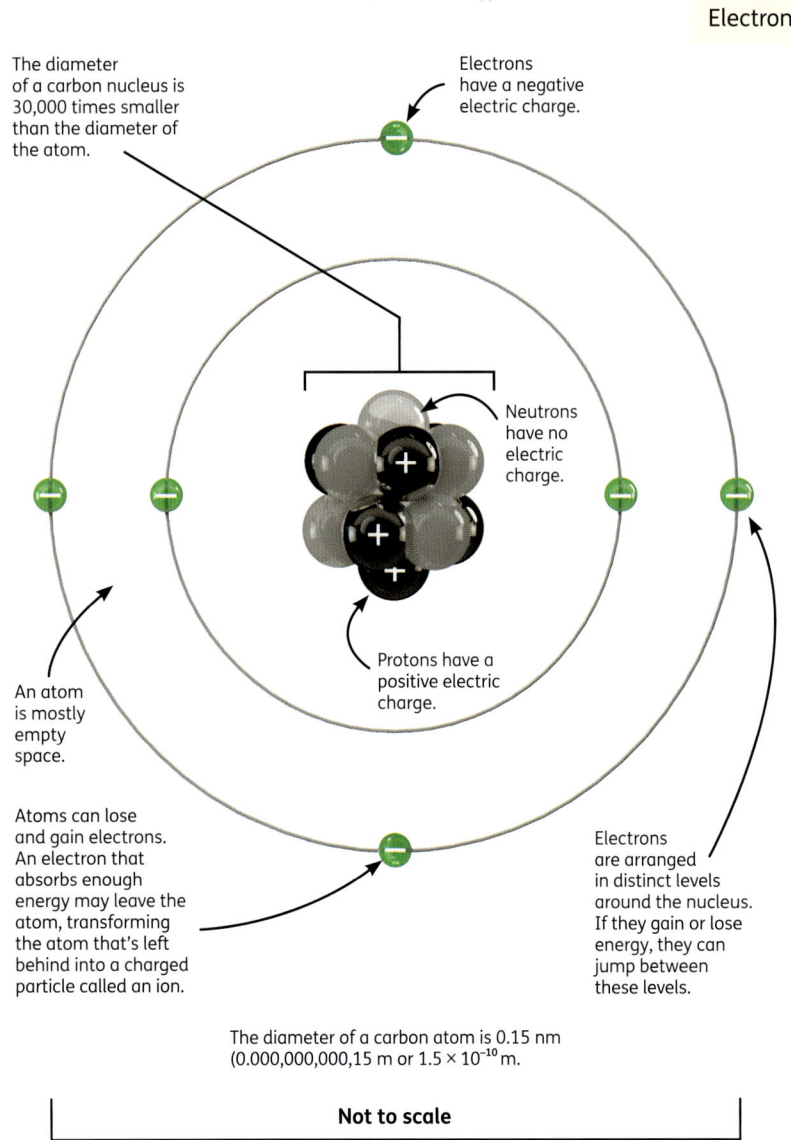

The diameter of a carbon nucleus is 30,000 times smaller than the diameter of the atom.

Electrons have a negative electric charge.

Neutrons have no electric charge.

Protons have a positive electric charge.

An atom is mostly empty space.

Atoms can lose and gain electrons. An electron that absorbs enough energy may leave the atom, transforming the atom that's left behind into a charged particle called an ion.

Electrons are arranged in distinct levels around the nucleus. If they gain or lose energy, they can jump between these levels.

The diameter of a carbon atom is 0.15 nm (0.000,000,000,15 m or 1.5×10^{-10} m.

Not to scale

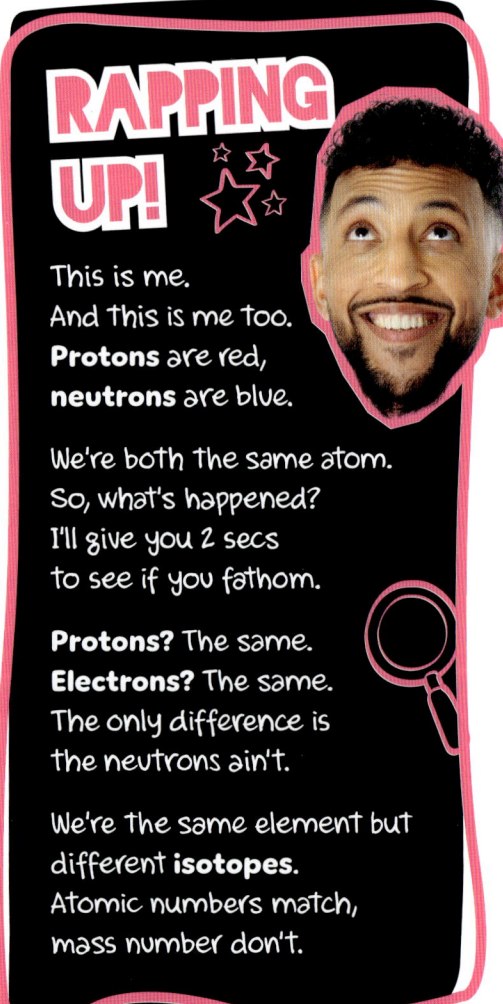

RAPPING UP!

This is me.
And this is me too.
Protons are red,
neutrons are blue.

We're both the same atom.
So, what's happened?
I'll give you 2 secs
to see if you fathom.

Protons? The same.
Electrons? The same.
The only difference is
the neutrons ain't.

We're the same element but different **isotopes**.
Atomic numbers match,
mass number don't.

Atomic Structure

Maths skills

When numbers are smaller than 1 there are prefixes you can use.

m means milli or $\frac{1}{1,000}$ or 10^{-3}

0.001 m = 1 mm

μ means micro or $\frac{1}{1,000,000}$ or 10^{-6}

0.000,001 m = 1 μm

n means nano or $\frac{1}{1,000,000,000}$ or 10^{-9}

0.000,000,001 m = 1 nm

Representing atoms

The carbon atom in the diagram has six protons, six neutrons and six electrons.

The atomic number is 6.

The mass number is 6 + 6 = 12.

The symbol for carbon is C.

You can represent the carbon atom like this:

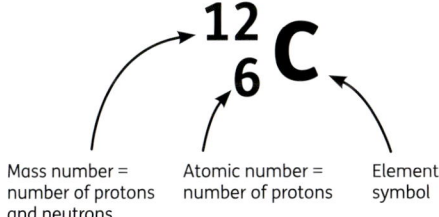

Mass number = number of protons and neutrons

Atomic number = number of protons

Element symbol

Isotope symbols

We can use symbols rather than writing out the name of an isotope in full. For example, the symbol for carbon-14 is:

$^{14}_{6}C$

This shows it has 6 protons and a total of 14 protons and neutrons. The number of neutrons is 14 − 6 = 8.

Mass number and atomic number

Atoms of a particular element all have the same number of protons.

Atoms have no overall electric charge, so the number of electrons is equal to the number of protons.

The atomic number of an element is the number of protons in an atom of the element.

The mass number is the total number of protons and neutrons in the atom.

Isotopes

The number of neutrons in an element can vary. An atom of the same element that has a different number of neutrons is an isotope of the element.

Three isotopes of carbon occur naturally. They all have the same number of protons and electrons. Carbon-12 has 6 neutrons, carbon-13 has 7 neutrons and carbon-14 has 8 neutrons.

They have the same chemical properties but have different masses. Carbon-12 and carbon-13 are stable but carbon-14 is unstable.

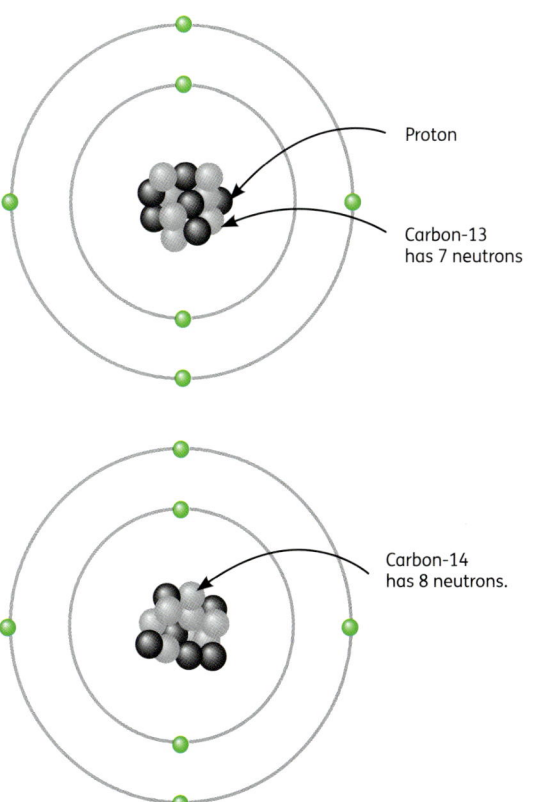

Proton

Carbon-13 has 7 neutrons

Carbon-14 has 8 neutrons.

Atomic Structure

Radioactive Decay and Nuclear Radiation

Key facts

- Some nuclei are unstable and emit radiation in a random process.
- The four types of ionising radiation emitted by radioactive nuclei are **alpha particles**, **beta particles**, neutrons and **gamma rays**.
- The changes that take place during radioactive decay can be shown in a nuclear equation.

Radioactive decay

Some atomic nuclei are unstable. The nucleus emits radiation to become more stable. This is a random process called radioactive decay.

The decay may cause a change in the atomic number and the mass number.

When the atomic number changes, a different element is formed.

The rate at which a source of unstable nuclei decays is its **activity**. It is measured in **becquerels** (Bq).

The number of decays recorded each second by a detector, such as a Geiger-Müller tube, is the count-rate.

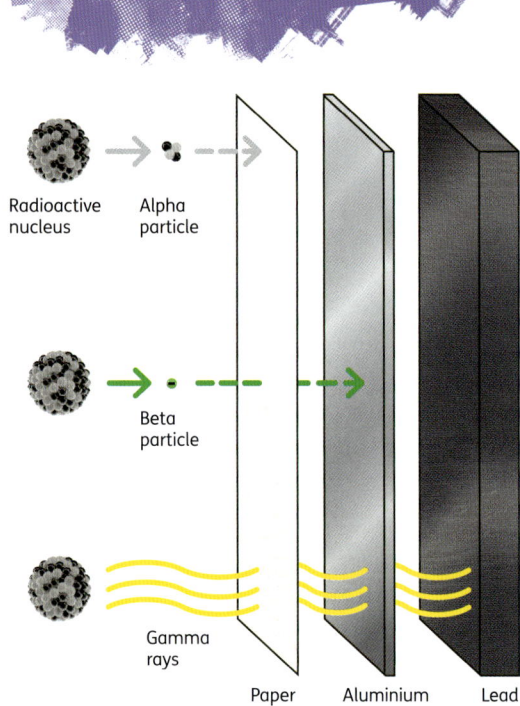

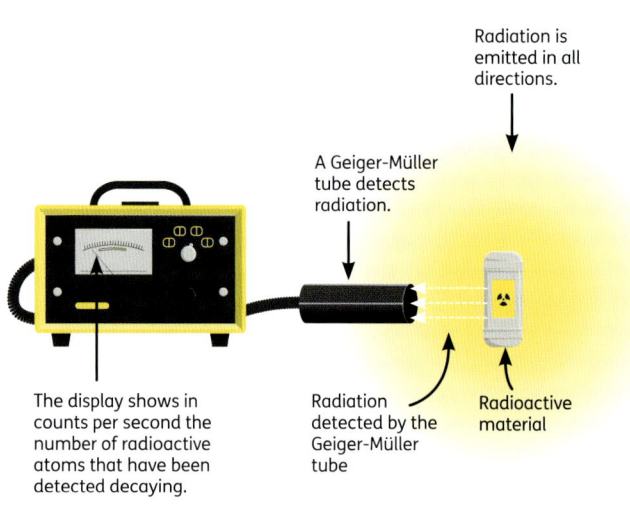

Radiation	What it is	Symbol	Effect on mass during decay	Effect on atomic number during decay
alpha (α)	helium nucleus: 2 protons and 2 electrons	$^{4}_{2}He$	decreases by 2	decreases by 2
beta particle (ß−)	high-speed electron	$^{0}_{-1}e$	stays the same	increases by 1
gamma ray (γ)	electromagnetic radiation	γ	stays the same	stays the same
neutron (n)	subatomic particle	$^{1}_{0}n$	decreases by 1	stays the same

Atomic Structure   51

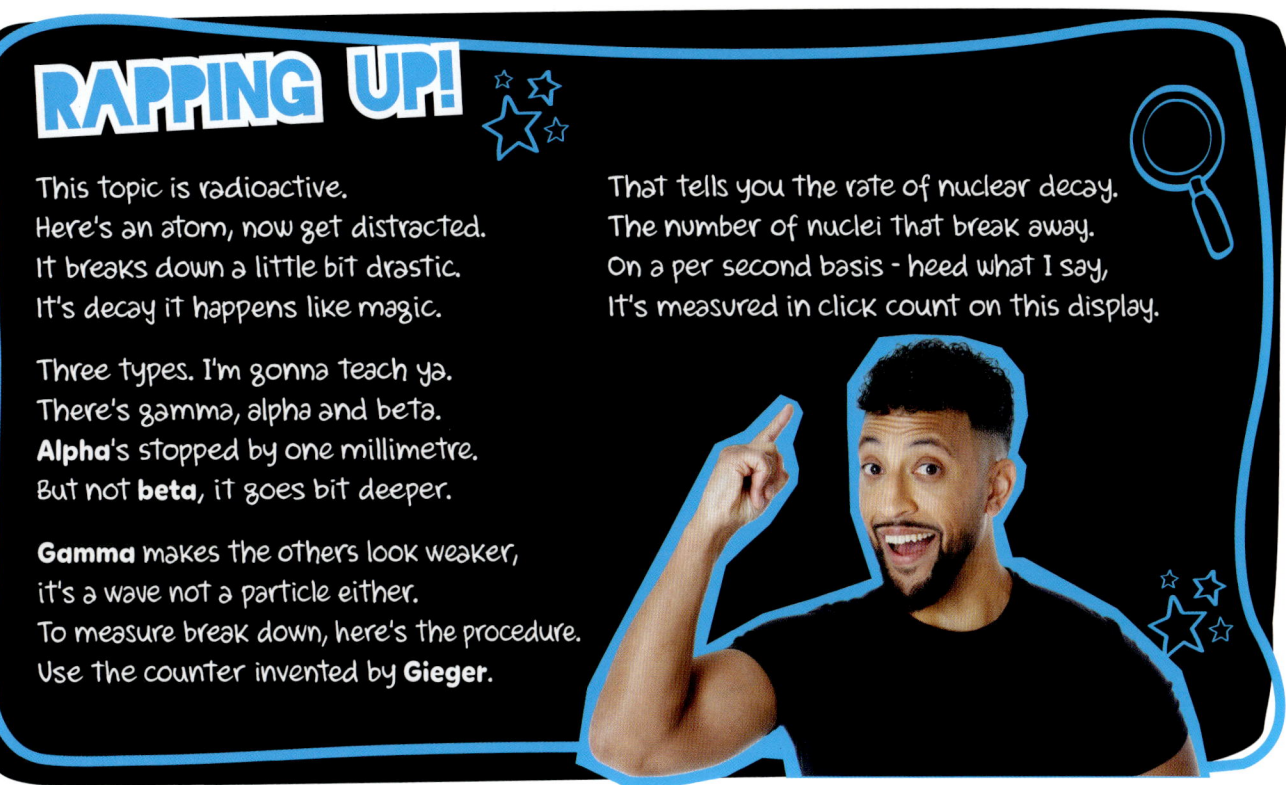

RAPPING UP!

This topic is radioactive.
Here's an atom, now get distracted.
It breaks down a little bit drastic.
It's decay it happens like magic.

Three types. I'm gonna teach ya.
There's gamma, alpha and beta.
Alpha's stopped by one millimetre.
But not **beta**, it goes bit deeper.

Gamma makes the others look weaker,
it's a wave not a particle either.
To measure break down, here's the procedure.
Use the counter invented by **Gieger**.

That tells you the rate of nuclear decay.
The number of nuclei that break away.
On a per second basis – heed what I say,
It's measured in click count on this display.

Nuclear equations

Nuclear equations are used to represent radioactive decay.

Alpha decay

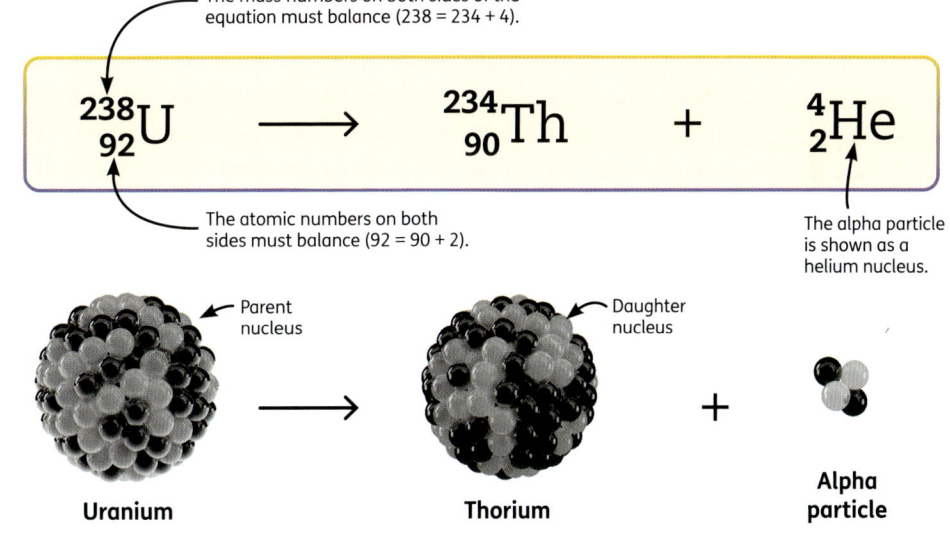

The mass numbers on both sides of the equation must balance (238 = 234 + 4).

$$^{238}_{92}U \longrightarrow \, ^{234}_{90}Th + \, ^{4}_{2}He$$

The atomic numbers on both sides must balance (92 = 90 + 2).

The alpha particle is shown as a helium nucleus.

Parent nucleus — Uranium
Daughter nucleus — Thorium
Alpha particle

Beta decay
In beta decay, a neutron turns into a proton and emits a high-speed electron.

A beta particle is written with −1 because it has a negative charge – the opposite of the positive charge carried by protons.

$$^{14}_{6}C \longrightarrow \, ^{14}_{7}N + \, ^{0}_{-1}e$$

Six protons — Seven protons

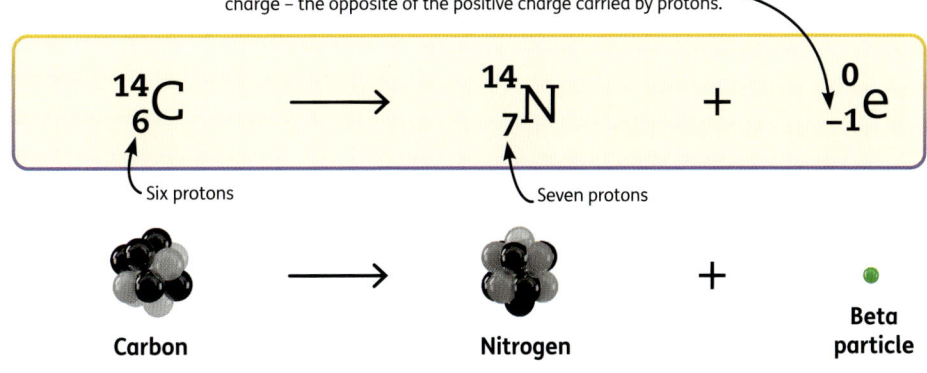

Carbon   Nitrogen   Beta particle

Atomic Structure

Half-life and Contamination

Key facts

- The half-life of a radioactive isotope is the time it takes for the half of the nuclei in a sample of the isotope to decay.
- Contamination occurs when radioactive material enters or gets onto an object or a person's body.
- Irradiation is when an object or a person is exposed to a radioactive material that is outside the body.

Half-life

The **half-life** of a radioactive isotope is also the time it takes for the count rate (or activity) from a sample containing the isotope to fall to half its initial level.

Radioactive decay is random – you cannot predict when a particular nucleus will decay. But, because there is a very large number of atoms in a sample, you can predict how long it will take for half of the nuclei to decay.

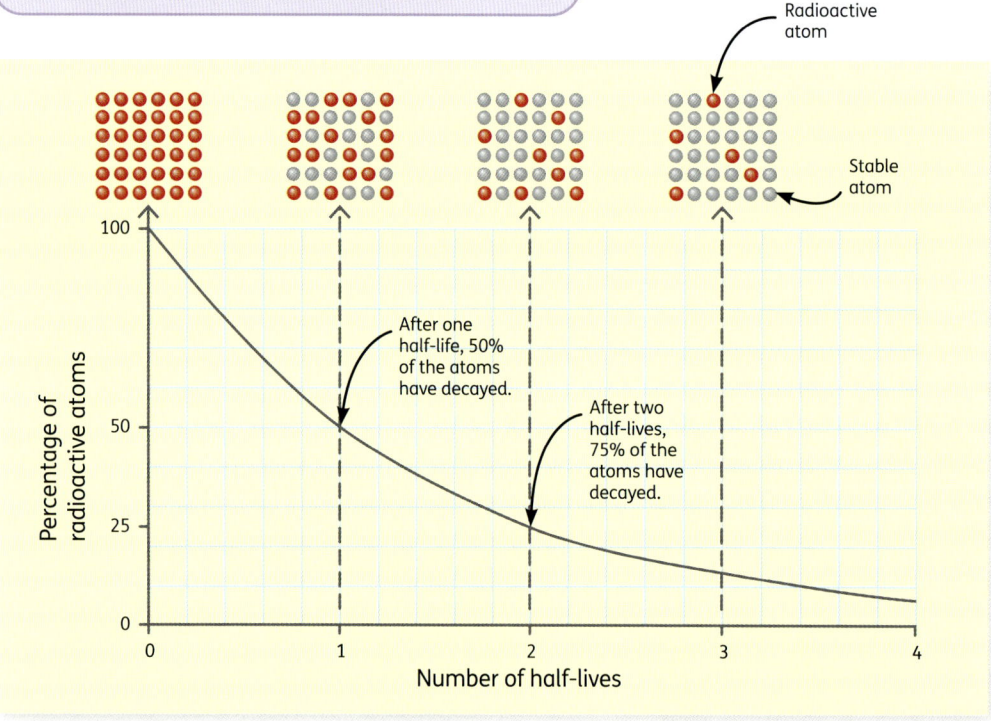

Maths skills

Determining half-life from a graph
You can determine the half-life of a radioactive isotope from a graph of activity of a sample of the isotope against time. Activity is on the vertical axis and time is on the horizontal axis.

1. Choose two points on the activity (vertical) scale of the graph. One value should be half of the other value.
2. Draw horizontal lines from these points to the graph.
3. Then draw vertical lines from where the horizontal lines meet the graph, down to the time axis.
4. Work out the time between the two lines on the time axis – this is the half-life.

Atomic Structure

Contamination

Radioactive **contamination** is when a person gets particles of radioactive material on their skin or inside their body. Objects can also be contaminated.

As the radioactive atoms decay, the person is exposed to ionising radiation. Sources with a short half-life are the most dangerous as they can release huge amounts of ionising radiation.

The diagram shows how a person can become contaminated.

Contamination

- Inhaling radioactive dust or smoke contaminates the lungs.
- Swallowed material can contaminate digestive organs and enter the bloodstream.
- Touching radioactive material can contaminate the skin.

Irradiation

Irradiation is the process of exposing an object to nuclear radiation.

The irradiated object does not become radioactive.

Irradiation stops as soon as the radioactive source is removed.

The diagram shows how a person can be irradiated.

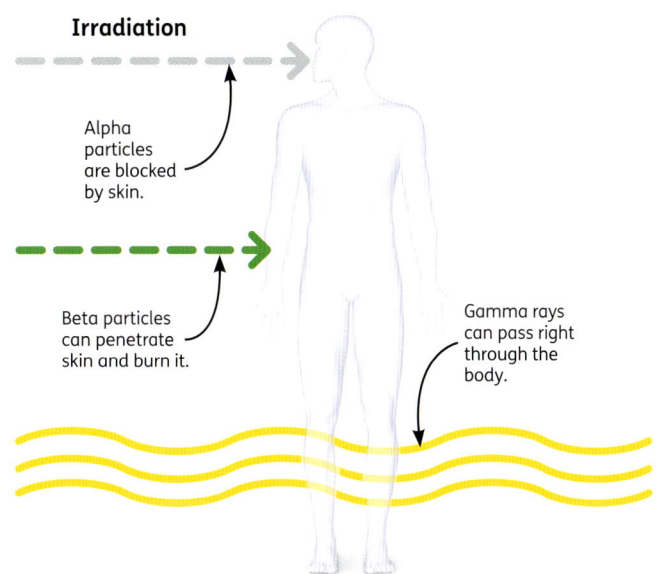

Irradiation
- Alpha particles are blocked by skin.
- Beta particles can penetrate skin and burn it.
- Gamma rays can pass right through the body.

RAPPING UP!

Radioactive decay is a random process.
Take a look at this and see if you notice.
I've got 10 trillion **nuclei**,
they break down anytime like mitosis.

We measure the breakdown here as count rate
using a **Geiger Muller** tube.
It counts each nuclear break down.
Then shows on the screen I'm showing to you.

Now you might have heard about **half-life**.
That's the amount of time that will pass by
when a substance count rate halves.
Time how long and plot on this graph.

In the example I'm showing you here,
the count rate here's in view.
If we take a ruler to half that
We can see the half-life is two!

Safety precautions

The precautions needed to stay safe when working with radioactive material depend on the material's half-life and what type of radiation it emits. The most dangerous sources are those with a short half-life as they can release large amounts of radiation in a short time.

When working with radioactive material, there are three main ways to stay safe which reduce the dose of radiation received.

- Limit the time spent near the radioactive source.
- Increase the distance from the source, for example, by handling sources with tongs.
- Use shielding to block radiation, for example, face masks and gloves for alpha particles and lead screens for gamma rays.

Hazards and Uses of Radiation

Key facts

- Background radiation is present all of the time and comes from natural and artificial sources.
- There are many uses of ionising radiation, for example in smoke detectors and for sterilising medical equipment.
- There are many medical uses of ionising radiation, including diagnosing and treating cancer.

Background radiation

The main sources of background radiation are shown in the pie chart.

Radon gas is released when radioactive isotopes in some rocks decay. In the UK, the percentage of background radiation from radon is about 50 per cent. This can be much higher in areas where there are granite rocks, such as south-west England.

The background radiation in the environment is monitored by scientists using Geiger-Müller tubes. The background radiation level is subtracted from measurements of radiation from radioactive materials so that the radioactivity of the material alone can be measured.

People in some jobs, such as astronauts, pilots and cabin crew, are exposed to higher levels of cosmic rays because they have less shielding from the Earth's atmosphere.

Different isotopes

Radioactive isotopes have a very wide range of half-lives, ranging from a fraction of a second to billions of years.

When choosing a radioactive isotope for medical uses, the half-life should be long enough for the diagnosis to be carried out, but short enough so that the patient is not exposed unnecessarily to radiation.

Isotope	Use
Iodine-131/Iodine-123	Thyroid diagnosis
Actinium-225	Prostate tumours
Carbon-11/Fluorine-19	Traces glucose in brain
Gallium-67	Scans for tumours
Selenium-75	Scans pancreas
Krypton-81m/Xenon-133	Lung ventilation scan
Strontium-81	Scans bones
Mercury-197	Kidney scan
Iron-59	Bone marrow function
Phosphorus-32	Detects eye tumours

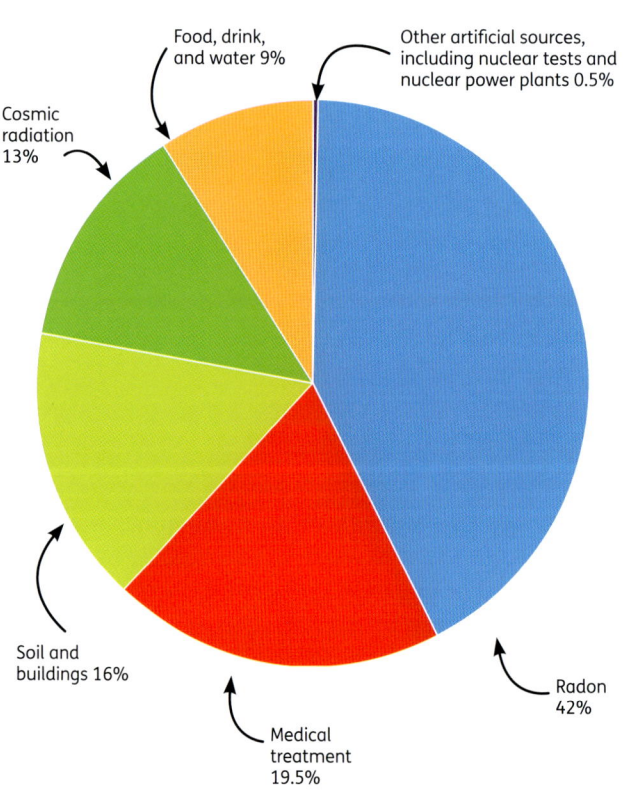

Estimates of worldwide sources of background radiation

Atomic Structure

Uses of radioactive isotopes

Smoke detectors contain a source of alpha particles, americium-241. The alpha particles emitted ionise the air between two plates, completing a circuit. Smoke particles bind to the ionised particles, breaking the circuit, which sets off the alarm.

The thickness of paper can be measured by passing beta particles through the paper to a detector. Some of the particles will be absorbed by the paper. The thickness of the paper is determined by measuring the amount of radiation that passes through.

Irradiating food and surgical equipment exposes the objects to high-energy gamma rays to kill microorganisms. This prevents decay in the food without affecting the taste of the food.

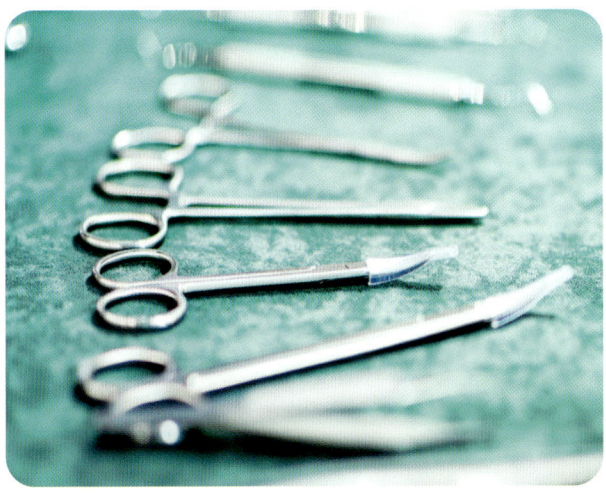

Positron emission tomography (PET) scanning involves radioactive isotopes being attached to another molecule and injected into the body. For example, the radioactive isotope fluorine is attached to glucose molecules. Glucose is used by all cells, so doctors can see where there are active tumours, or areas that are less active, such as a brain that is affected by Alzheimer's disease.

Internal radiotherapy involves the implantation of a radioactive source into the body beside a tumour. A source of alpha particles is usually used, so that only the immediate area around the source receives a dose of radiation.

Radiotherapy uses narrow beams of radiation that are aimed at cancer cells in the body from many different angles. This maximises the radiation dose received by the cancer cells and minimises the dose received by surrounding cells.

Diagnosing disease can be done by injecting a radioactive substance, called a tracer, which emits gamma rays into the body.
The tracer accumulates more strongly in areas with cancer cells. The gamma rays are detected by a gamma camera. The image shows where a tracer has accumulated in bones affected by cancer.

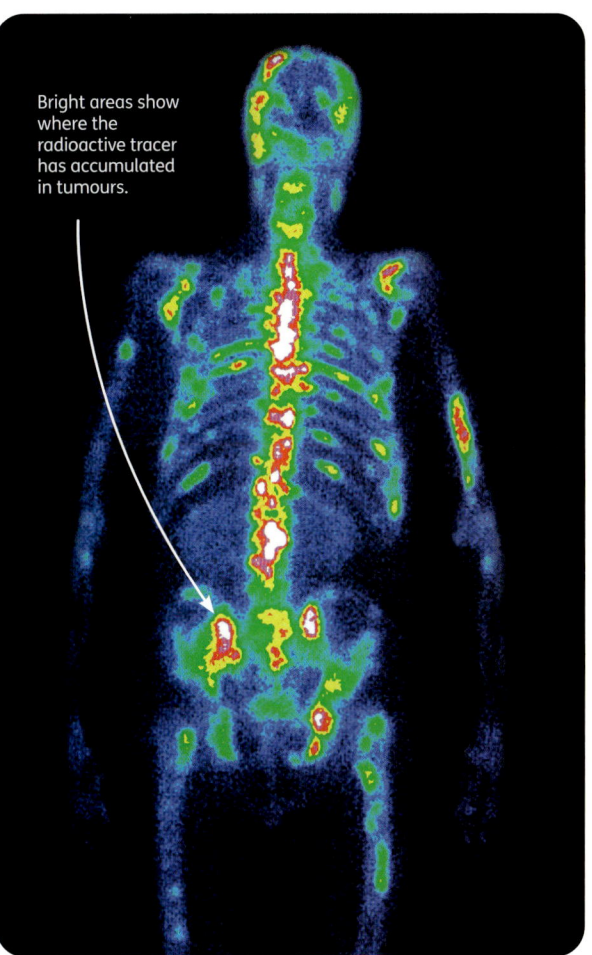

Bright areas show where the radioactive tracer has accumulated in tumours.

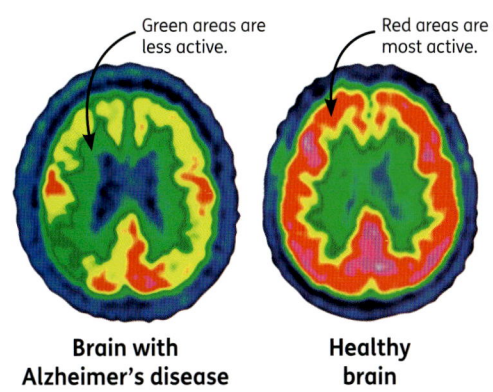

Green areas are less active.

Red areas are most active.

Brain with Alzheimer's disease

Healthy brain

Atomic Structure

Nuclear Fission and Fusion

Key terms

- **Nuclear fission** is the splitting of a large unstable nucleus into two or more smaller nuclei.
- **Nuclear fusion** is the joining (fusing) of two small nuclei to make a larger nucleus.
- In both processes a large amount of energy is released.
- Nuclear fission can be controlled using rods of materials that absorb neutrons, such as boron, cadmium, silver, hafnium, or indium.

Nuclear fission

Nuclear fission is the splitting of a large and unstable nucleus such as uranium or plutonium. Fission rarely happens spontaneously. Usually, a neutron is absorbed by the nucleus.

Energy is released by the fission reaction. All the products of nuclear fission have kinetic energy.

The products of nuclear fission are radioactive.

Much more energy is released from uranium than from burning the same mass of coal or natural gas.

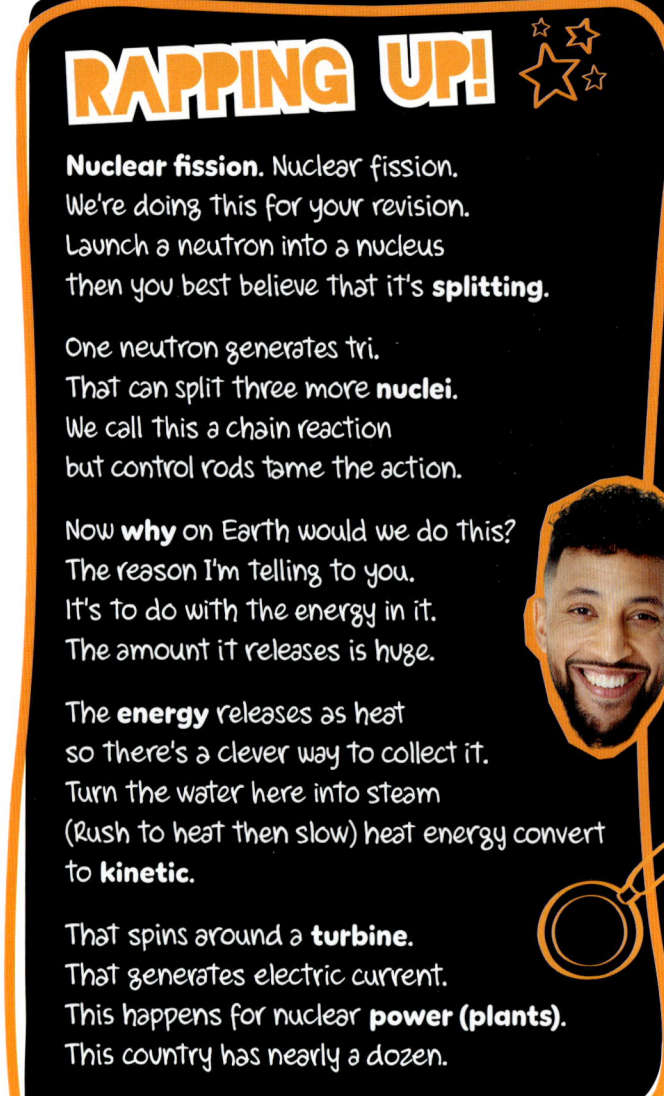

RAPPING UP!

Nuclear fission. Nuclear fission.
We're doing this for your revision.
Launch a neutron into a nucleus
then you best believe that it's **splitting**.

One neutron generates tri.
That can split three more **nuclei**.
We call this a chain reaction
but control rods tame the action.

Now **why** on Earth would we do this?
The reason I'm telling to you.
It's to do with the energy in it.
The amount it releases is huge.

The **energy** releases as heat
so there's a clever way to collect it.
Turn the water here into steam
(Rush to heat then slow) heat energy convert to **kinetic**.

That spins around a **turbine**.
That generates electric current.
This happens for nuclear **power (plants)**.
This country has nearly a dozen.

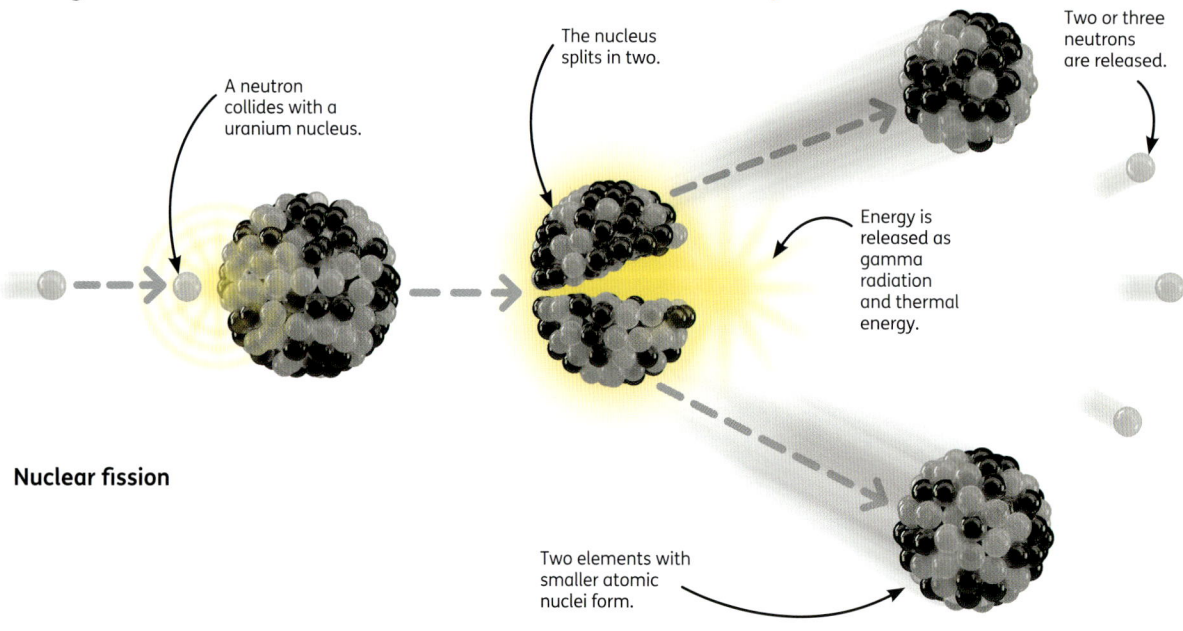

Nuclear fission

Chain reaction

The neutrons may go on to start a **chain reaction**.

The diagram shows a controlled chain reaction where only one neutron goes on to cause another fission. This is what happens in a nuclear reactor. The other neutrons are absorbed by control rods in the core of the nuclear reactor.

The explosion caused by a nuclear weapon is caused by an uncontrolled chain reaction. All of the neutrons go on to cause another fission.

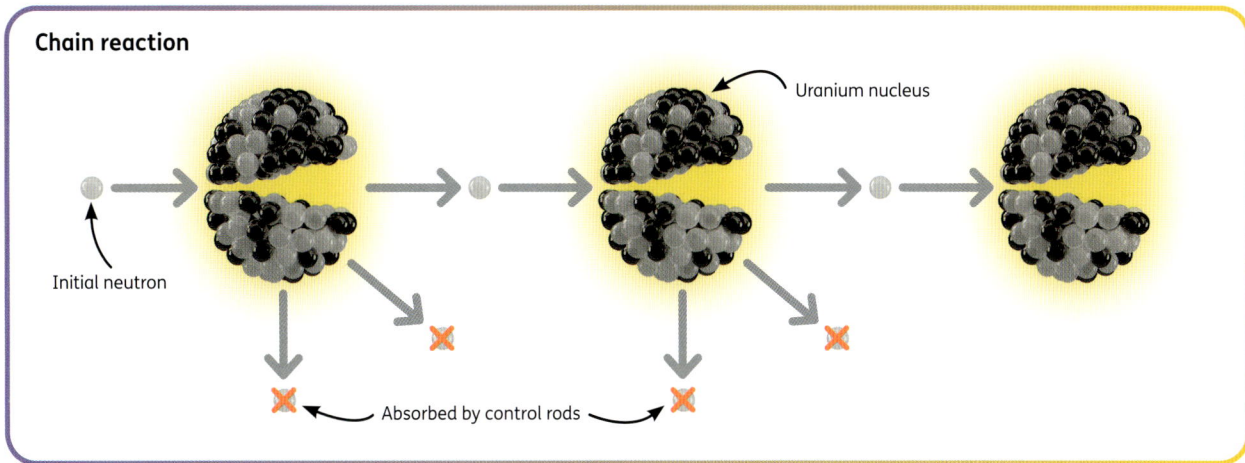

Nuclear fusion

Nuclear fusion is the joining together of two small nuclei to create a larger nucleus, while energy is released.

A small amount of mass is converted to energy.

Fusion is the energy source for stars.

Fusion in stars takes place at very high temperatures and pressures because the nuclei repel each other as they both have positive charges. These conditions mean that it is very difficult to build a fusion reactor on Earth.

Fusion of hydrogen to form helium

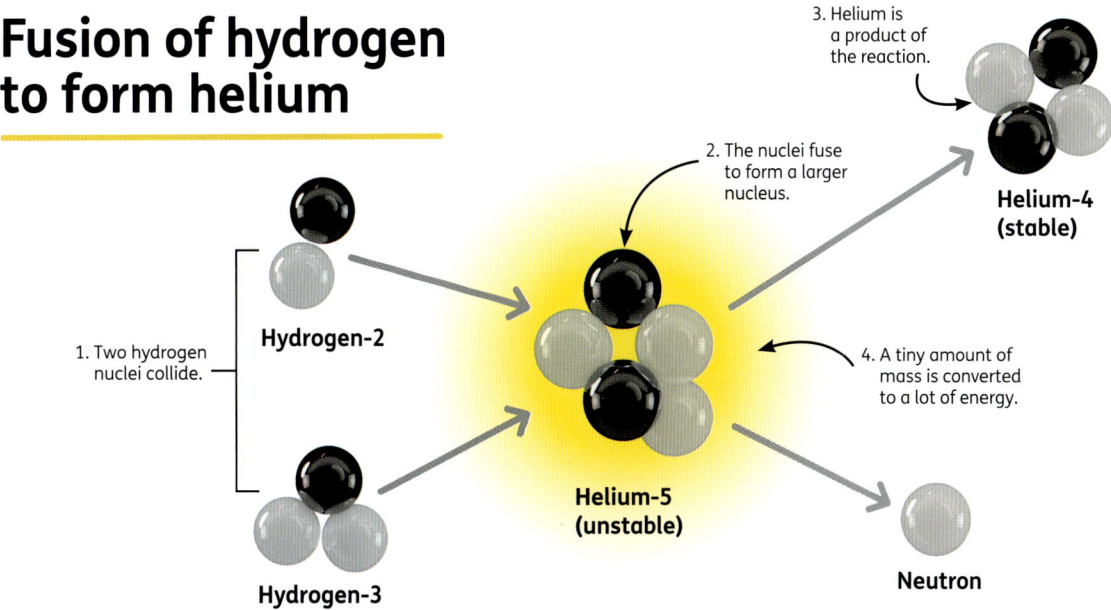

Brain Booster

Atomic Structure Recap Quiz

 Find a pen and paper and work through these revision questions.

1. Potassium has 19 protons and 20 neutrons. Its element symbol is K. Write potassium in symbol form with the atomic number and mass number.

2. Explain what an isotope is.

3. Explain the difference between the plum pudding model and the nuclear model of the atom.

4. Balance each nuclear equation.

   a) $^{222}_{86}\text{Rn} \rightarrow\ ^{\square}_{\square}\text{Po} + ^{4}_{2}\text{He}$ b) $^{137}_{55}\text{Cs} \rightarrow\ ^{\square}_{55}\text{Ba} + ^{0}_{\square}\text{e}$

5. Give the name of the radiation emitted in each equation in question 4.

6. The table shows the activity of a sample of technetium-99m.

Time (hours)	0	2	4	6	8	10	12
Activity (Bq)	400	320	250	200	160	128	100

   Use the data in the table to work out the half-life of technetium-99m.

7. Explain what background radiation is.

8. What type of radiation is used in smoke detectors?

9. Give **two** uses of radioactive isotopes in medicine.

10. Explain the difference between a controlled and an uncontrolled chain reaction.

Check your answers on page **109**.

Forces

At the end of this chapter, you should be able to:

- ✓ Explain the difference between scalar and vector quantities.
- ✓ Calculate weight and work done.
- ✓ Explain how the shape of an object can be changed by forces.
- ✓ Calculate spring constant.
- ✓ Describe the effect of moments on a balanced object.
- ✓ Describe how levers and gears work.
- ✓ Calculate pressure.
- ✓ Calculate distance travelled, speed and acceleration.
- ✓ Use distance–time and velocity–time graphs.
- ✓ Explain what terminal velocity is.
- ✓ Explain and apply Newton's laws of motion.
- ✓ Describe the factors affecting braking distance.

Forces and their Interactions

Key facts

- A force is a push or a pull that changes the motion or shape of an object.
- Scalar quantities have magnitude only. Temperature is a scalar quantity.
- Vector quantities have magnitude and direction. They can be represented by arrows in diagrams.
- Weight (in N) = Mass (in kg) × Gravitational field strength (in N/kg)

Scalars and vectors

Examples of scalar quantities are mass, distance, speed and energy.

Examples of vector quantities are force, displacement, velocity and acceleration.

You can represent a vector quantity by an arrow. The length of the arrow gives the magnitude, and the direction of the arrow gives the direction of the vector.

You can find the resultant of one of more forces by drawing force diagrams showing the vectors. The vectors can either act in straight lines or at right angles. Here are some examples.

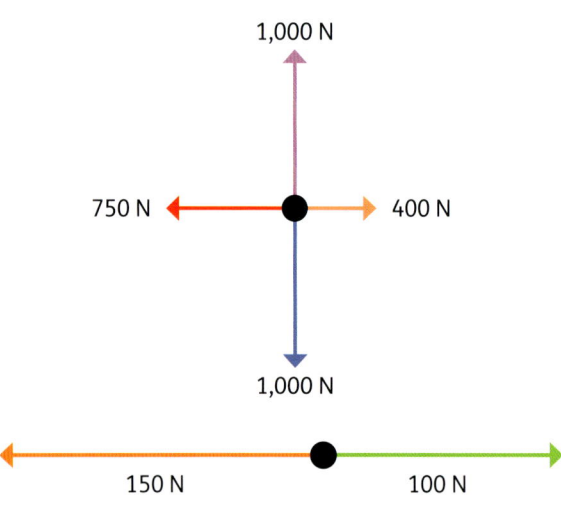

RAPPING UP!

This is **gravity**.
I'm now about to show you proof
from this penthouse floor.
I'm about to jump off from the roof.
Gravity acts on all objects with a mass.
The Earth is big, so the more gravity it has.

Gravity's a force that **pulls** all objects to each other.
I'm pulled to Earth, Sir Isaac Newton did discover.
My mass don't change whether I'm on Earth
or I'm in space,
But when on Earth, the gravity gives me a **weight**.

Weight makes me **accelerate** down towards the street,
But very soon I will reach a constant speed.
This is because **air resistance** matches gravity.
We call this speed the terminal velocity.

Nine point eight metres
per second squared on Earth.
Twenty-four point eight on Jupiter is even worse!
Acceleration due to gravity is g
Times by mass equals weight
here as you can see.

Forces

Gravity and weight

The force of **gravity** close to the Earth is due to the gravitational field around the Earth.

The weight of an object depends on the gravitational field strength at the point where the object is.

Weight is measured using a newton meter, which is a calibrated spring-balance.

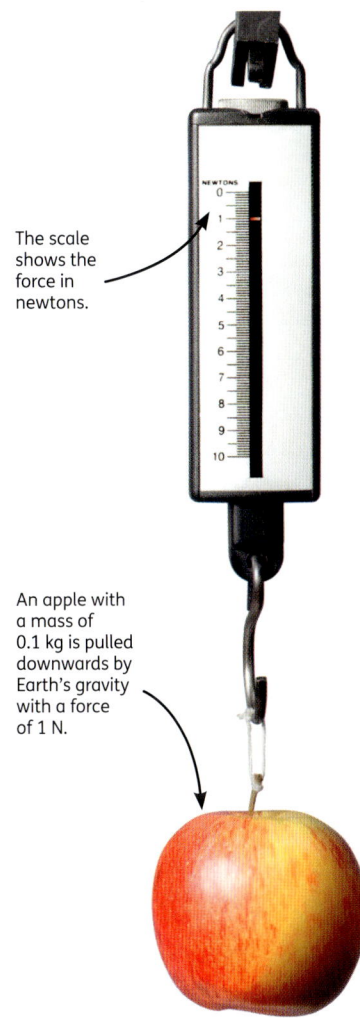

The scale shows the force in newtons.

An apple with a mass of 0.1 kg is pulled downwards by Earth's gravity with a force of 1 N.

Contact and non-contact forces

A force is a push or pull that acts on an object. All forces are either:

- Contact forces where the objects are physically touching.
- Non-contact forces where the objects are physically separated.

Examples of contact forces are friction, air and water resistance, tension and normal contact force.

Examples of non-contact forces are gravitational force, electrostatic force and magnetic force.

Kicking a ball is an example of a contact force.

The non-contact force of gravity acts on the skydiver.

Calculating weight

Question
Perseverance is a rover on Mars. It has a mass of 1,025 kg. Calculate Perseverance's weight on Mars. The gravitational field strength on Mars is 3.7 N/kg

Answer
Weight = Mass × Gravitational field strength

= 1,025 × 3.7

= 3,792.5 N = 3,800 N (2 s.f.)

Centre of mass

The weight of an object may be considered to act at a single point. This is referred to as the object's centre of mass.

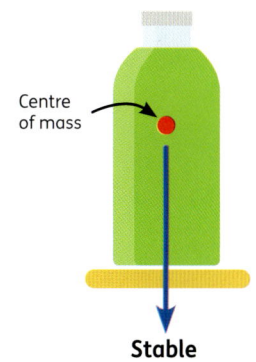

Centre of mass

Stable

Resultant Forces and Work Done

> **Key facts**
> - A **resultant force** is the single force that has the same effect as two or more forces acting together on an object.
> - **Work done** (in J) = Force (in N) × Distance moved along the line of action of the force (in m)
> - 1 joule = 1 newton-metre

Finding resultant forces

There are several different forces acting on the rope. They act in straight lines in opposite directions in two pairs.

To work out the resultant force:

- When the forces act in the same direction, add them together.
- When the forces act in opposite directions, subtract one from the other.

When the forces are balanced, the resultant force is zero.

The resultant force on the tug-of-war teams is zero so the forces are balanced. There is no movement.

The dog and sledge are moving. The resultant force on the dog and sledge is zero. The dog and sledge will continue to move at the same velocity.

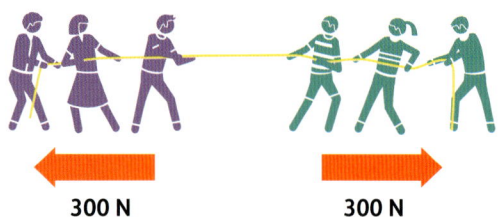

300 N   300 N

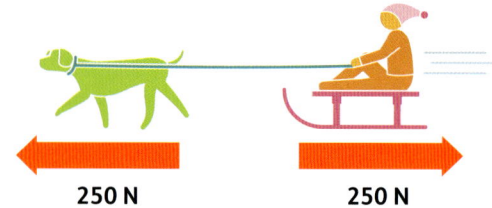

250 N   250 N

The weight of the sledge below and the normal contact force are equal and opposite. The vertical resultant force is zero.

The tension and friction are opposite but not equal. The tension is 750 N forwards and friction is 400 N backwards.

Resultant force = 750 − 400 = 350 N forwards, or to the left.

So the sledge will accelerate forwards.

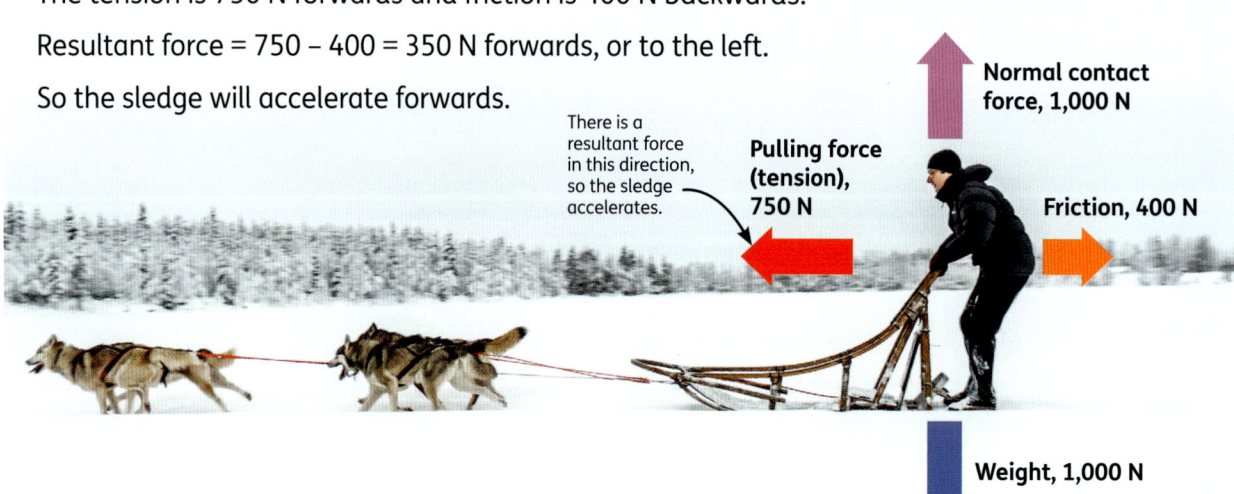

There is a resultant force in this direction, so the sledge accelerates.

Pulling force (tension), 750 N

Normal contact force, 1,000 N

Friction, 400 N

Weight, 1,000 N

Forces

Calculating resulting forces

Question
Two people push a piano. One person pushes it to the right with a force of 150 N. Another person pushes it to the left with a force of 200 N. Calculate the resultant force on the piano.

Answer
Draw a diagram showing the forces acting on the piano.

Subtract to find the resultant force:
200 N – 150 N = 50 N (to the left).

Work done

When a force causes an object to move through a distance, work is done on the object. The pulling force on the sledge does work on the sledge when the sledge moves.

You can use the equation to calculate the work done on an object.

1 joule of work is done when a force of 1 newton causes a displacement of 1 metre.
1 joule = 1 newton-metre.

Energy transfers and work done
Work is done whenever energy is transferred.

When work is done on the sledge, energy is transferred to the kinetic energy store of the sledge.

There is friction between the sledge's runners and the ground. Work is done against this frictional force. Energy is transferred from the kinetic energy store of the sledge by heating.

Calculating work done

Question
The sledge in the photo moves 50 m. The resultant force on the sledge is 350 N. Calculate the work done on the sledge.

Answer
Work done = Force × Distance moved

= 350 × 50

= 17,500 J or 17.5 kJ

This is also equal to 17,500 newton-metres (Nm).

Question
A person weighing 350 N climbs 3 m up a ladder.

How much work do they do?

Answer
Work done = Force × Distance moved

= 350 × 3

= 1,050 J

Question
You push a shopping trolley 4 m with a force of 14 N.

How much work do you do?

A force of 14 newtons acts continuously for 4 metres.

Answer
Work done = Force × Distance moved

= 14 × 4

= 56 J

Forces and Elasticity

Key facts

- **Elastic deformation** happens when a spring is stretched and then released and the spring returns to its original shape.
- **Inelastic deformation** happens when a material like modelling clay is stretched and then released and it does not return to its original shape.
- When you apply a force to a spring, it will extend or contract.
- The increase in length of an object is known as its extension.
- The extension of a spring is directly proportional to the force applied.
- Force (in N) = Spring constant (in N/m) × Extension (in m)

Deformation

Forces can deform (change the shape of) an object by stretching, bending or compressing it.

When a pair of forces push an object in opposite directions, this creates compression and squashes the object.

When a pair of forces pull an object in opposite directions, this creates tension and causes the object to stretch.

When more than two forces act on an object in different directions, they can bend the object.

Two or more forces are needed because the forces need to oppose each other. If there was only one force, the object would just move in the direction of that force.

Extension of an elastic object

The extension of an elastic object, such as a spring, is directly proportional to the force applied, provided that the limit of proportionality is not exceeded. The relationship also applies to the compression of an object.

A force that stretches (or compresses) a spring does work, and elastic potential energy is stored in the spring. The work done on the spring and the elastic potential energy stored are equal, as long as the spring is not inelastically deformed.

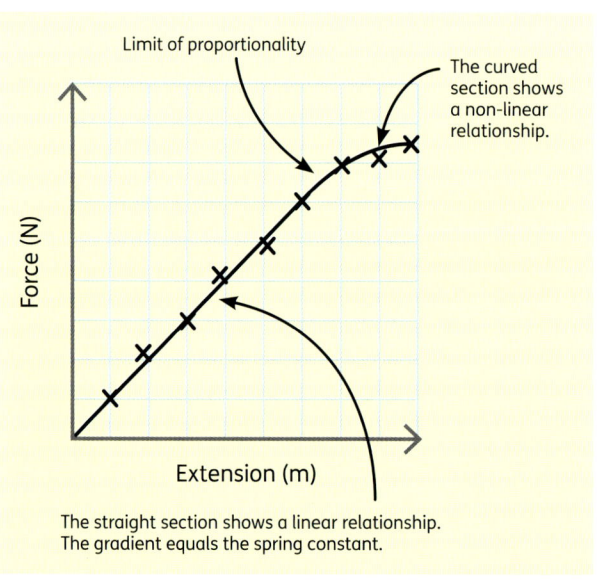

The straight section shows a linear relationship. The gradient equals the spring constant.

Calculating spring constant

Question
A spring is extended by 8 cm when a force of 4 N stretches it. Calculate the spring constant of the spring.

Answer
Extension = 8 cm = 0.08 m

Rearrange the equation to make spring constant the subject:

Spring constant = $\dfrac{\text{Force}}{\text{Extension}}$ = $\dfrac{4}{0.08}$ = 50 N/m

Question
A spring is extended by 15 cm when a force of 6 N stretches it. Calculate the spring constant of the spring.

Answer
Extension = 15 cm = 0.15 m

Rearrange the equation to make spring constant the subject:

Spring constant = $\dfrac{\text{Force}}{\text{Extension}}$ = $\dfrac{6}{0.15}$ = 40 N/m

Science skills

Investigating springs

You can use the equipment shown in the diagram to investigate how extension varies with force applied.

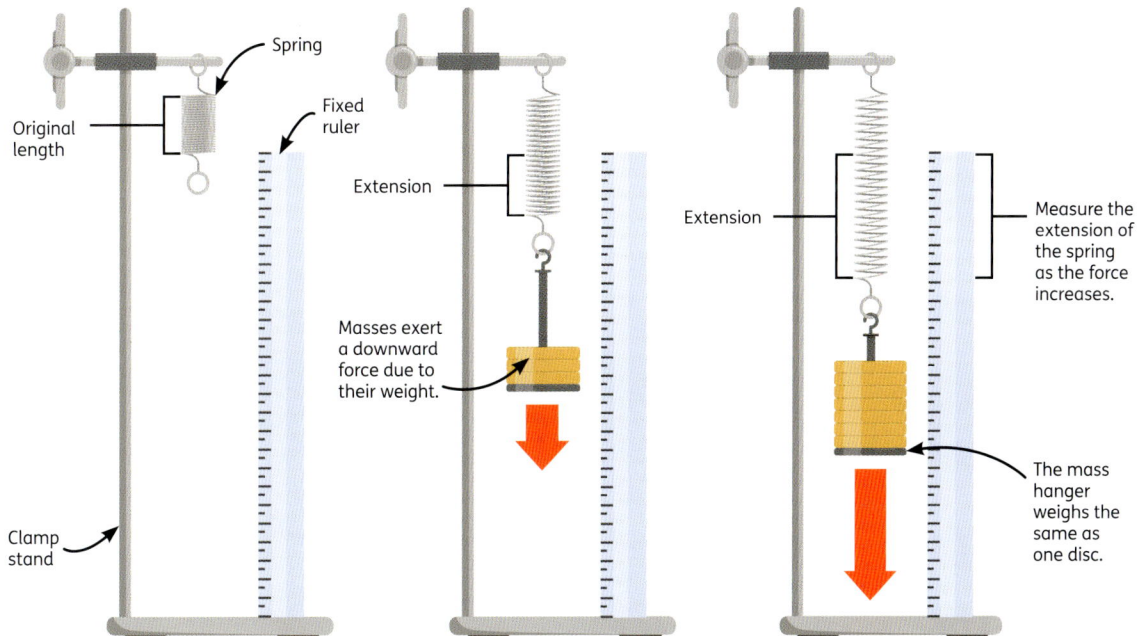

Hang a mass on the end of a spring. Record the mass and the extension. Increase the mass gradually. For each mass, record the extension.

Plot a graph of force against extension with force in newtons on the *y*-axis (remember to convert mass to newtons) and the extension of the spring on the *x*-axis. The graph should be a straight line through the origin. This shows that the extension is directly proportional to the force (if you double the force, the extension doubles). If you add too many masses, the limit of proportionality is reached and the extension is no longer directly proportional to the mass so the graph curves.

Moments, Levers and Gears

Key terms

- A **moment** is the turning effect of a force.
- Moment of a force (in Nm) = Force (in N) × Perpendicular distance from the pivot to the line of action of the force (in m)
- A **lever** is a simple machine that magnifies or reduces the effects of forces.
- A **gear** is a wheel with a toothed edge that transmits rotational forces.

Moments

A force or a system of forces may cause an object to rotate. If an object is balanced, the total clockwise moment about a pivot equals the total anticlockwise moment about that pivot.

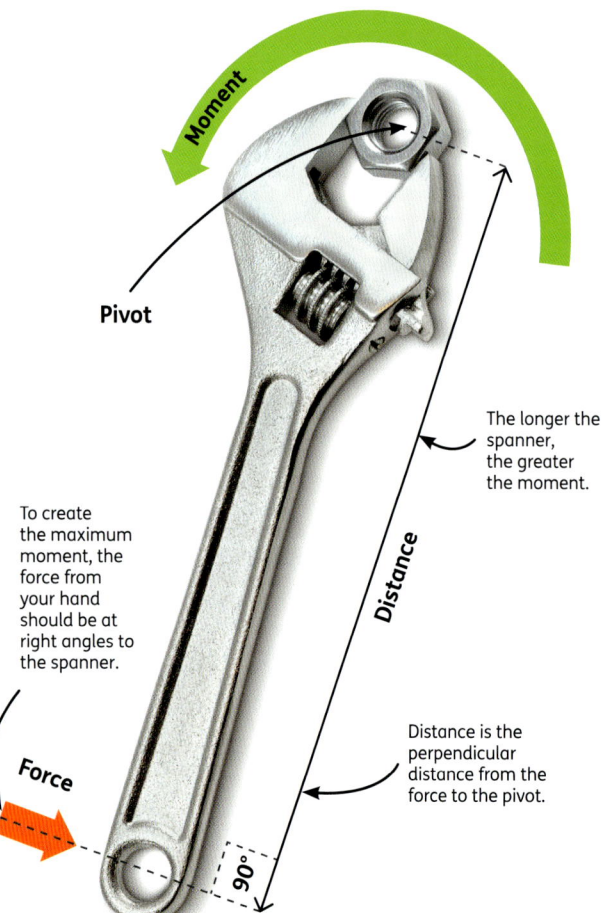

Calculating moments

Question
A force of 40 N is applied at the end of a spanner that is 30 cm long. Calculate the moment of the spanner.

Answer
Convert distance to metres: 30 cm = 0.3 m

Moment = Force × Perpendicular distance

= 40 × 0.3

= 12 Nm

Question
The seesaw is balanced. How far from the pivot is the person on the right?

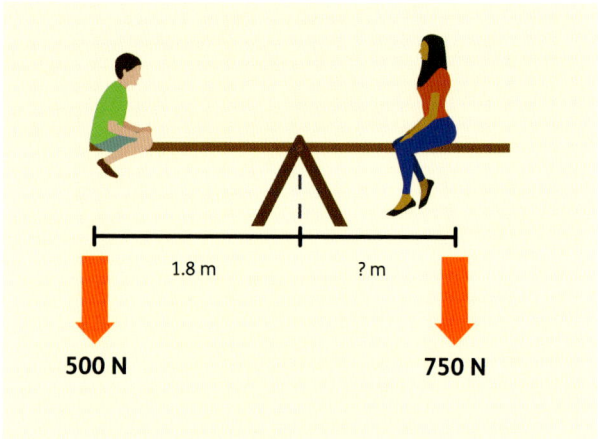

Answer
First work out the anticlockwise moment produced by the person on the left:

Anticlockwise moment = Force × Distance

= 500 × 1.8

= 900 Nm

As the seesaw is balanced, the anticlockwise and clockwise moments are equal.

Clockwise moment = 900 N/m = 750 × Distance

Rearrange the equation to make distance the subject:

Distance = $\dfrac{900}{750}$

= 1.2 m

Forces

Levers and gears

A simple lever and a simple gear system can both be used to transmit the rotational effects of forces.

Levers
A lever is a rigid object that can rotate around a fixed point called a pivot or a fulcrum.

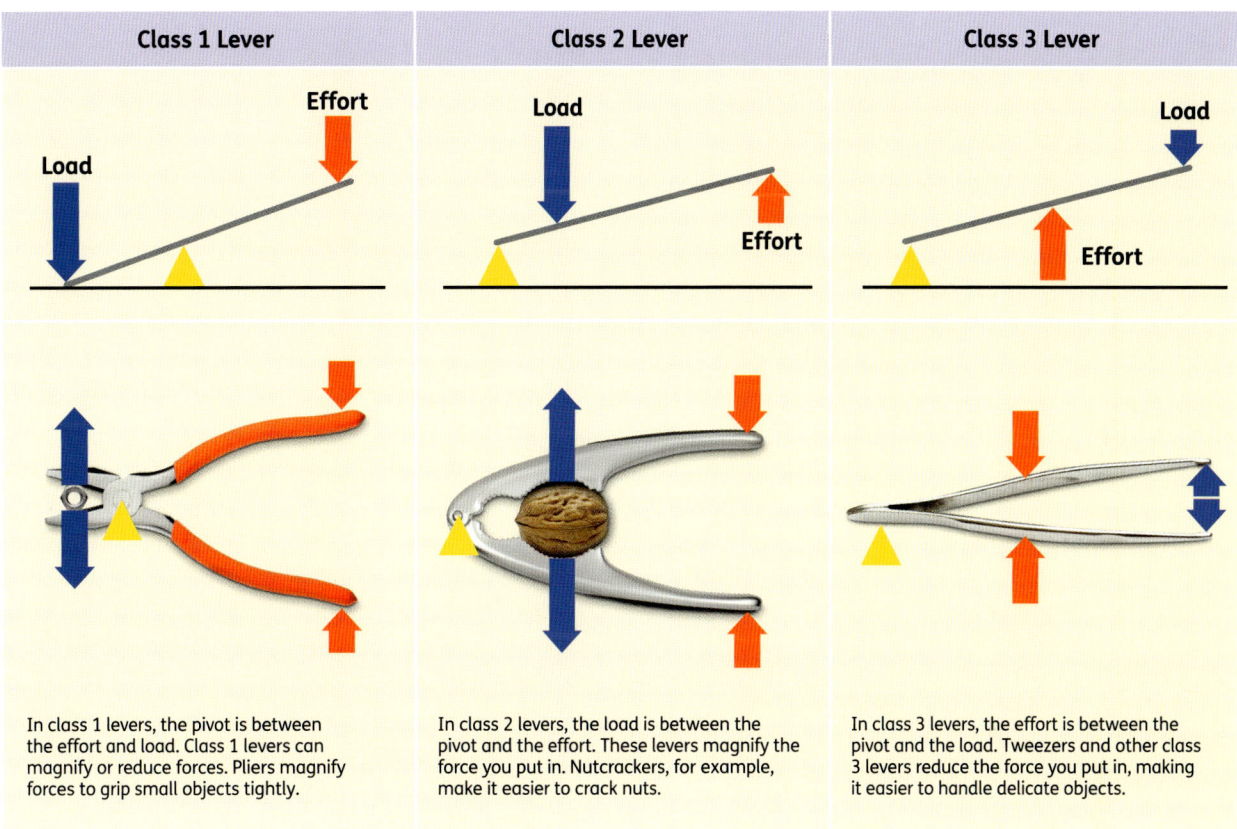

| Class 1 Lever | Class 2 Lever | Class 3 Lever |

In class 1 levers, the pivot is between the effort and load. Class 1 levers can magnify or reduce forces. Pliers magnify forces to grip small objects tightly.

In class 2 levers, the load is between the pivot and the effort. These levers magnify the force you put in. Nutcrackers, for example, make it easier to crack nuts.

In class 3 levers, the effort is between the pivot and the load. Tweezers and other class 3 levers reduce the force you put in, making it easier to handle delicate objects.

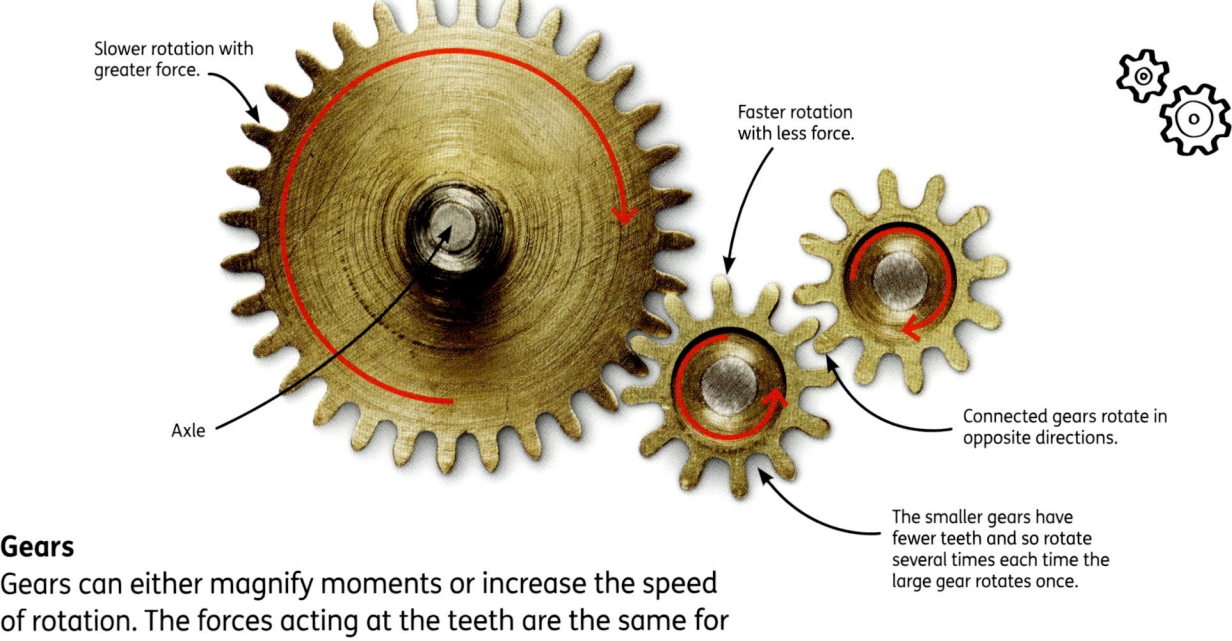

Gears
Gears can either magnify moments or increase the speed of rotation. The forces acting at the teeth are the same for all three gears, but the moments are different because the gears have different numbers of teeth.

Pressure in a Fluid

Key facts

- Pressure at surface of a fluid (in Pa) = $\dfrac{\text{Force normal to surface (in N)}}{\text{Area of surface (in m}^2\text{)}}$
- Pressure in a fluid increases with depth and with density.
- Pressure due to liquid = Height × Density × Gravitational field strength
- Total pressure underwater equals pressure due to the water plus pressure due to the atmosphere.
- Atmospheric pressure is the pressure on Earth's surface caused by the weight of air in the atmosphere.
- Atmospheric pressure falls with increasing altitude.

Pressure

A fluid can be either a liquid or a gas. The pressure in fluids causes a force normal (at right angles) to any surface.

The pressure in fluids increases with depth and density. So the pressure at the sea bed is greater than the pressure near the surface. Divers have to be careful how quickly they come up to the surface so that they do not suffer from a condition known as decompression sickness. At high pressure under water, more nitrogen dissolves into the bloodstream. If a diver surfaces too quickly, the dissolved nitrogen forms bubbles in the body.

When you press a balloon with your thumb the pressure is much lower than when you apply the same force with a pin. The pressure with a pin is much higher as it is spread over a much smaller area.

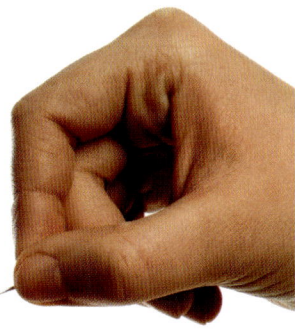
Applying a force with a tiny surface area creates high pressure and bursts the balloon.

Calculating pressure

Question
A cabin bag with a weight of 80 N is placed on a flat surface. Its base is 0.5 m long by 0.4 m wide. Calculate the pressure exerted by the bag on the surface.

Answer
Calculate the surface area of the bag in square metres.

Area = 0.5 × 0.2
     = 0.1 m²

Pressure = $\dfrac{\text{Force}}{\text{Area}}$ = $\dfrac{80}{0.1}$ = 800 Pa

Question
A box with a weight of 60 N is placed on a flat surface. Its base is 0.2 m long by 0.3 m wide. Calculate the pressure exerted by the box on the surface.

Answer
Calculate the surface area of the box in square metres.

Area = 0.2 × 0.3
     = 0.06 m²

Pressure = $\dfrac{\text{Force}}{\text{Area}}$ = $\dfrac{60}{0.06}$ = 1,000 Pa

Atmospheric pressure

The atmosphere is a layer of air around the Earth that is thin relative to the size of the Earth.

There are air molecules all around you that collide with surfaces, creating atmospheric pressure. This pressure acts on us all the time and in all directions, even though we cannot see or feel it.

When a glass on top is turned upside down, the card stays in place, held by atmospheric pressure.

Weight
Water in glass
Card
The force from atmospheric pressure is greater than the downward force of the water's weight.
Atmospheric pressure

The number of air molecules above a surface decreases as the height of the surface above ground level increases. The weight of air above you decreases with increasing height. As height increases there is always less air above a surface than there is at a lower height. So atmospheric pressure decreases with an increase in height.

Atmospheric pressure at sea level is about 100,000 Pa (or 100 kPa).

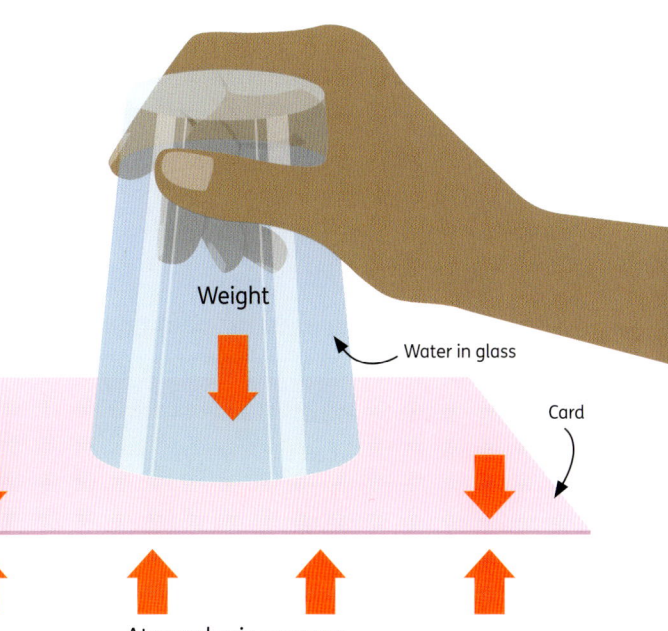

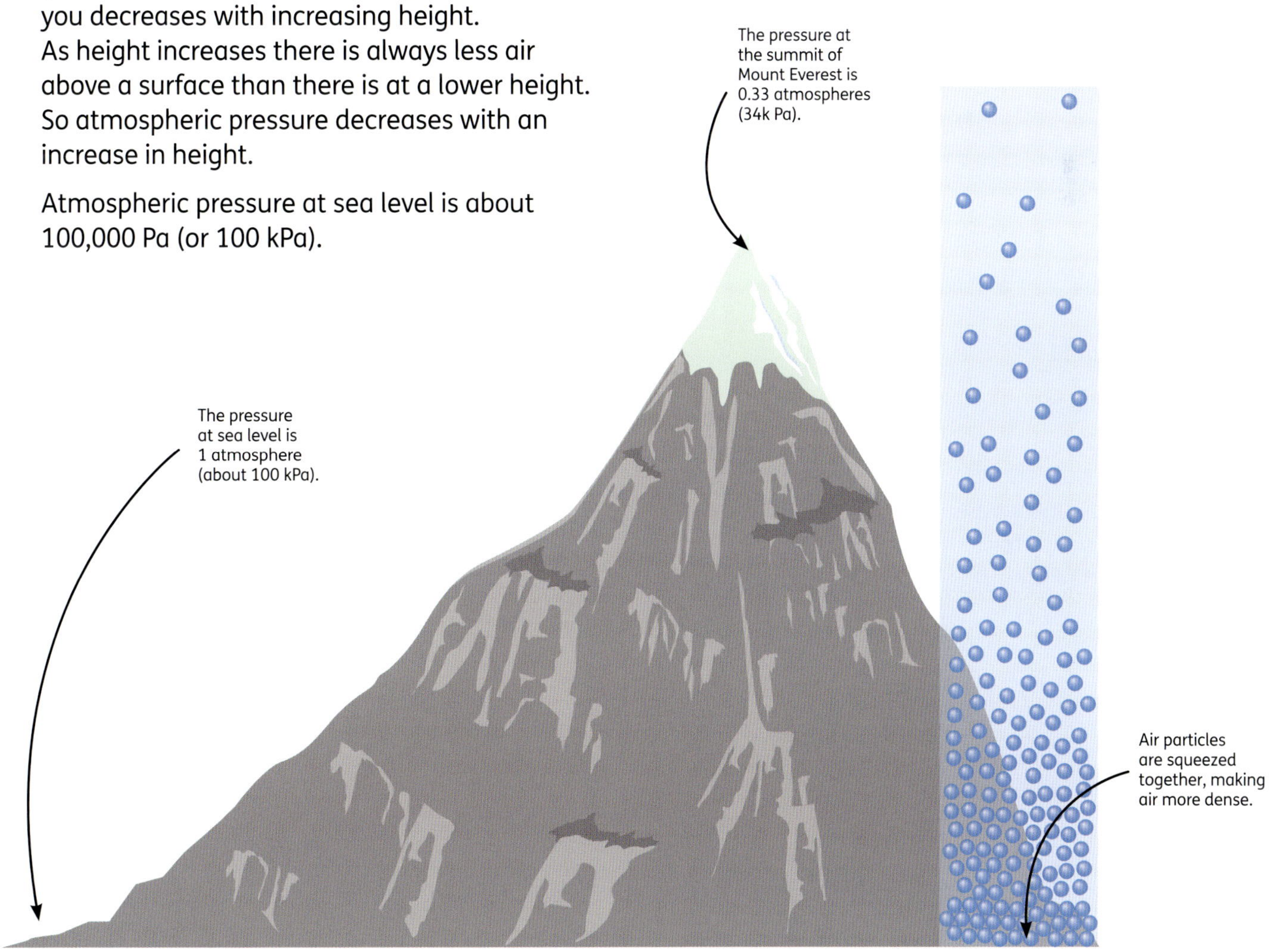

The pressure at the summit of Mount Everest is 0.33 atmospheres (34k Pa).
The pressure at sea level is 1 atmosphere (about 100 kPa).
Air particles are squeezed together, making air more dense.

Distance, Displacement and Speed

Key facts

- Distance and speed are scalar quantities because they only have a magnitude.
- Displacement is a vector quantity because it has both magnitude and a direction.
- Distance travelled (in m) = (Average) speed (in m/s) × Time (in s)

Distance and displacement

Displacement is the distance, measured in a straight line, from the start point to the finish point and the direction of that straight line.

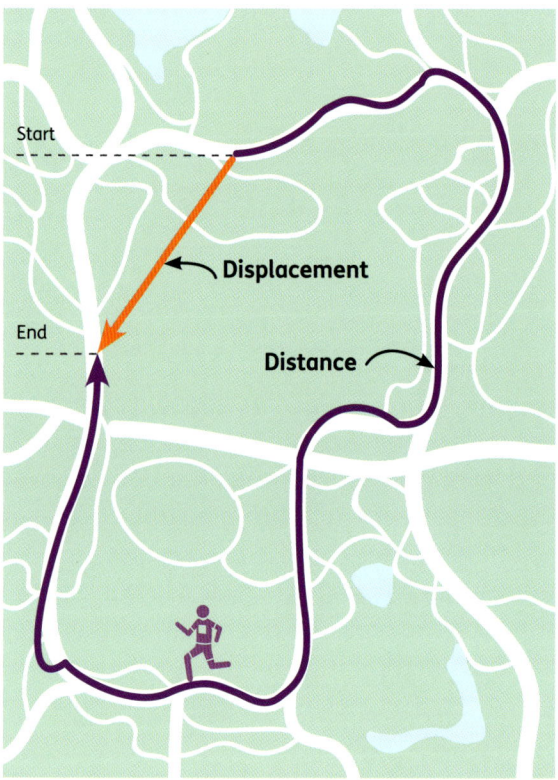

Speed

The speed of a moving object is rarely constant. When people walk, run or travel in a car their speed is constantly changing. The speed at which a person can walk, run or cycle depends on many factors including age, terrain, fitness and distance travelled. The speed of sound and the speed of the wind also vary.

Typical speeds

The bar chart shows some typical speeds. A typical value for the speed of sound in air is 330 m/s.

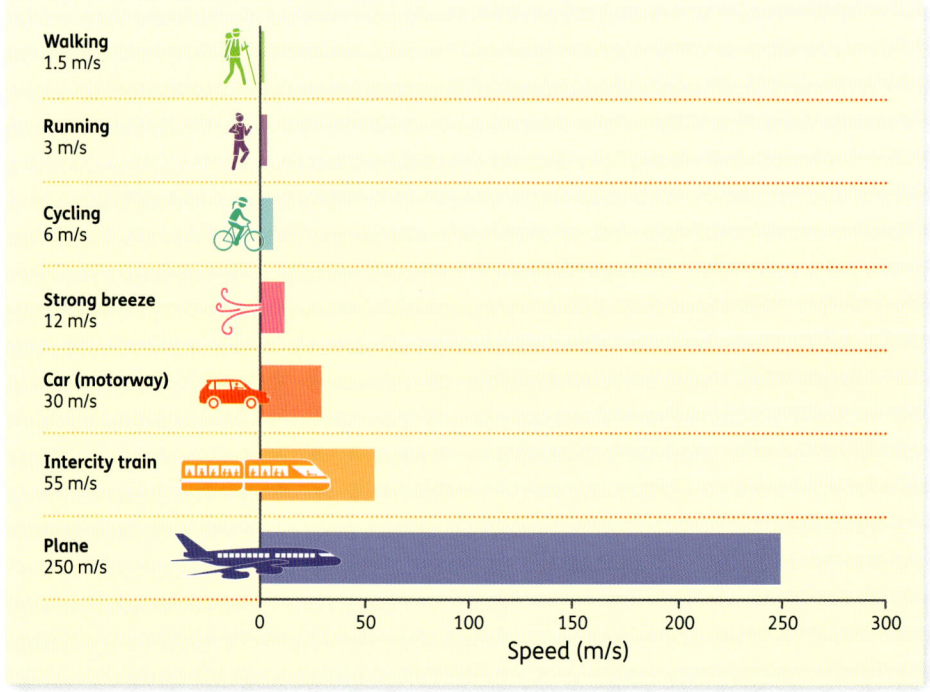

Calculating distance

Question
A car travels at 15 m/s for 50 seconds. How far does the car travel?

Answer
Distance = Speed × Time

= 15 × 50

= 750 m

Question
A train travels at 160 km/h for 2 hours. How far does the train travel?

Answer
Distance = Speed × Time

= 160 × 2

= 320 km

Calculating speed

Question
A runner completes a 400 m race in 50 seconds. What is their average speed?

Answer
Rearrange the equation for distance to make speed the subject of the equation:

$$\text{Average speed} = \frac{\text{Total distance}}{\text{Time}} = \frac{400}{50} = 8 \text{ m/s}$$

Question
A rowing crew completes a 6.8 km race in 18 minutes. What is their average speed? Give your answer in m/s.

Answer
6.8 km = 6,800 m

18 minutes = 60 × 18 seconds

= 1,080 seconds

Rearrange the equation for distance to make speed the subject of the equation:

$$\text{Average speed} = \frac{\text{Total distance}}{\text{Time}}$$

$$= \frac{6,800}{1,080}$$

= 6.3 m/s

Measuring speed

You can use the equipment shown in the diagram to measure speed.

The speed is calculated by dividing the length of the card by the time on the timer.

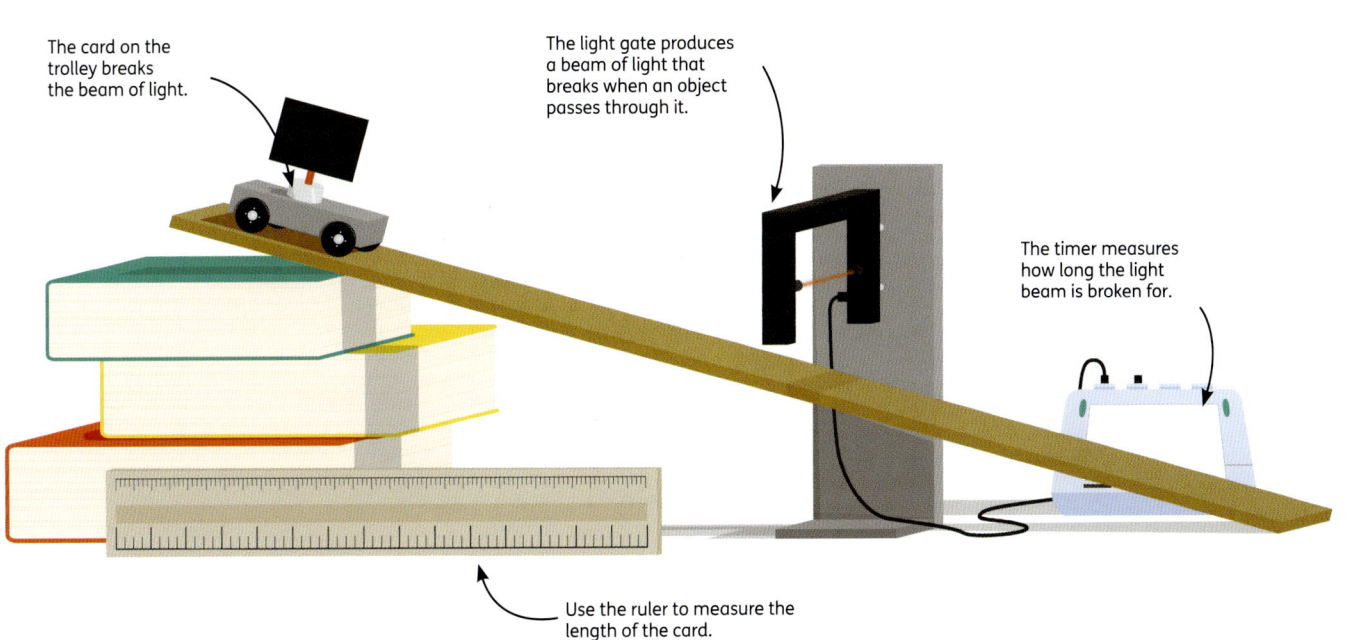

The card on the trolley breaks the beam of light.

The light gate produces a beam of light that breaks when an object passes through it.

The timer measures how long the light beam is broken for.

Use the ruler to measure the length of the card.

Velocity and Distance–Time Graphs

Key facts

- The velocity of an object is its speed in a given direction. Velocity is a vector quantity.
- A distance–time graph shows the journey of an object travelling in a straight line.
- The gradient of a distance–time graph gives speed.

Drawing a distance–time graph

Question
A car travels 200 m in 10 s. It then travels a further 400 m in the next 40 s.

Draw a distance–time graph for the car's journey.

Answer
The total distance travelled is 200 + 400 = 600 m.

The total time is 10 + 40 = 50 s.

Draw axes with distance on the vertical axis going from 0 m to 600 m and time on the horizontal axis going from 0 s to 50 s.

Draw a line for the first part of the journey from (0, 0) to (10, 200).

Draw a line for the second part of the journey from (10, 200) to (50, 600)

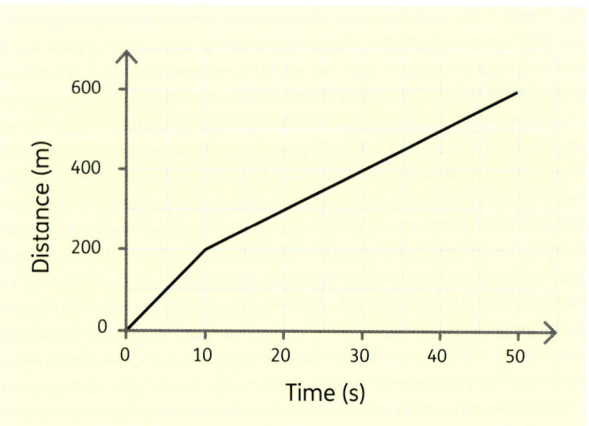

RAPPING UP!

Working out **speed** – it's easy you'll find:
It's distance divided by time.
Keep it in mind that these units feature:
Time is **seconds**; distance is **metres**.

Last one left is your **secret weapon**.
Know that speed is metres per second.
Rearrange all of these and you'll find
Distance equals speed by the time.

Speed? Velocity? What's their description?
They're not the same; I'll explain the difference.
Speed's **scalar**, velocity's **vector**.
Speed's how fast, without the direction.

Done with speed, now **acceleration**.
They're not the same, here's a calculation:
Speed change here, and time below there.
Unit's like speed but this time it's squared.

Forces

Interpreting distance–time graphs

On a distance–time graph:

- The steeper the line, the faster an object is moving.
- A curved line has a changing gradient, which means an object is changing speed.
- A horizontal line means an object is stationary.

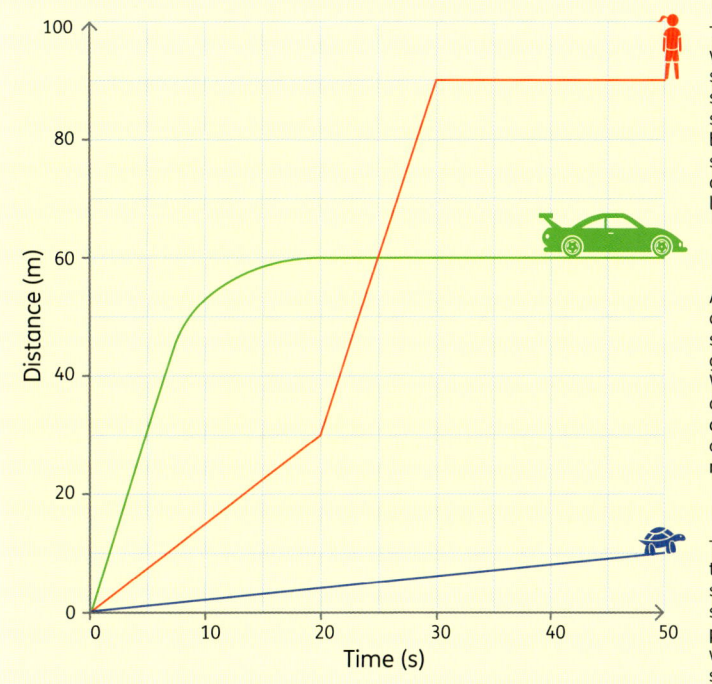

This person starts walking at a constant speed, but after 20 seconds she suddenly speeds up – she must be running. After 10 seconds of running, she comes to a stop and the line remains horizontal.

At first the car travels quickly at a constant speed, but then it gradually slows. When it reaches a distance of 60 m, its distance travelled stops changing, so the car must have stopped.

The low gradient of the tortoise's line shows that it walks slowly. The line is perfectly straight, which means that its speed is not changing.

Maths skills

Determining speed from a distance–time graph

The speed of an object can be calculated from the gradient of its distance–time graph.

Question
Look at the distance–time graph below. What was the speed of the car during the last 40 s of the journey?

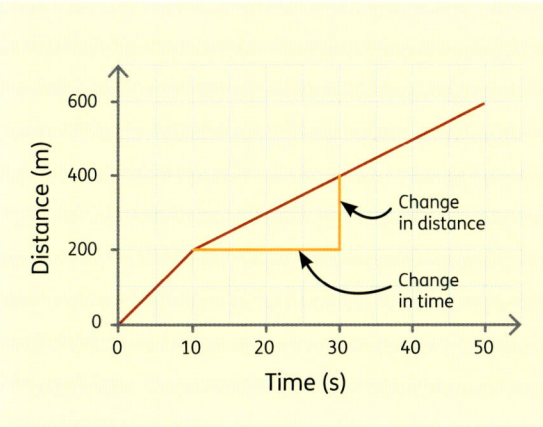

Answer
Find the gradient of the line between 10 s and 50 s.

Draw a right-angled triangle under any part of the line (the gradient is the same between 10 and 50 s). The triangle's vertical side is the change in distance. The horizontal side is the change in time.

Work out both values.

Change in distance = 400 m − 200 m = 200 m

Change in time = 30 s − 10 s = 20 s

Divide the change in distance by the change in time to find the speed.

$$\text{Speed} = \frac{\text{Change in distance}}{\text{Change in time}} = \frac{200}{20} = 10 \text{ m/s}$$

Acceleration

Key facts

- Acceleration (in m/s^2) = $\dfrac{\text{Change in velocity (in m/s)}}{\text{Time (in s)}}$
- The gradient of a velocity–time graph gives acceleration.
- (Final velocity (in m/s))^2 − (Initial velocity (in m/s))^2 = 2 × Acceleration (in m/s^2) × Distance (in m)

Calculating acceleration

An object that slows down is decelerating.

Question
A car is travelling at 30 m/s on a motorway. It slows down to 15 m/s in 20 seconds to leave the motorway on an exit ramp.
What is the acceleration of the car?

Answer
Acceleration = $\dfrac{\text{Change in velocity}}{\text{Time}}$

= $\dfrac{15 - 30}{20}$ = −0.75 m/s^2

The acceleration is negative because the car is slowing down.

Velocity–time graphs

A velocity–time graph shows how an object's velocity changes over time.

Slopes with a straight line represent uniform acceleration or deceleration, but curved lines represent changing acceleration or deceleration. Horizontal lines represent constant velocity.

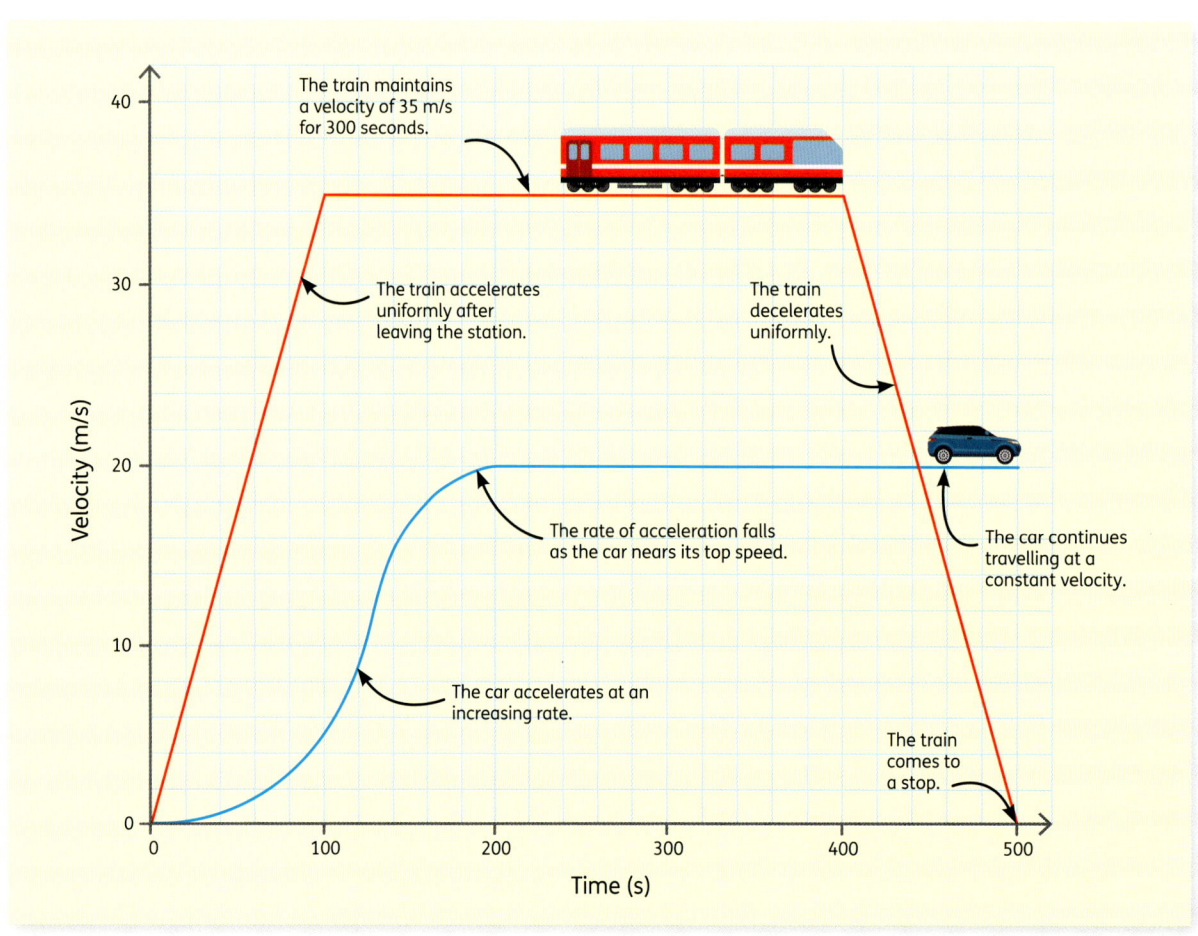

Forces

Calculating acceleration from a velocity–time graph

Question
The graph shows a car's journey. What was the car's acceleration between 10 and 30 seconds?

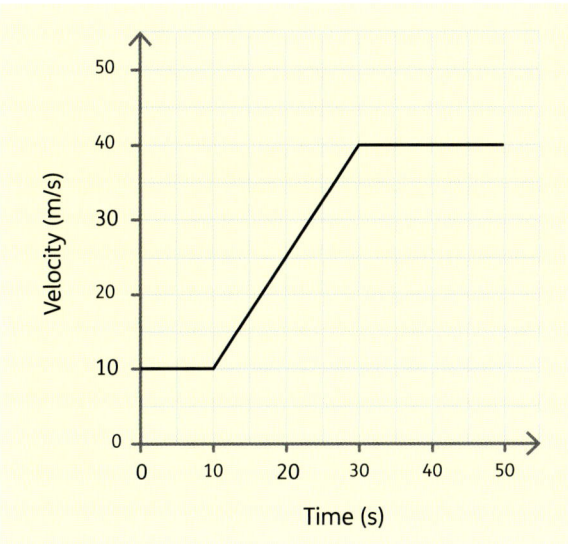

Answer
Draw a triangle under the sloped part of the graph.

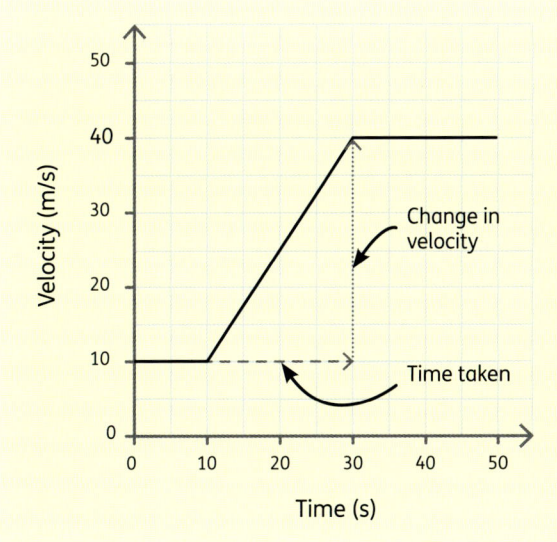

Change in velocity = 40 − 10 = 30 m/s

Change in time = 30 − 10 = 20 s

Acceleration = $\frac{30}{20}$ = 1.5 m/s²

Terminal velocity

Near the Earth's surface, any object falling freely under gravity has an acceleration of about 9.8 m/s².

The velocity–time graph shows a skydiver's journey.

In the first part of the graph, the skydiver's weight is larger than the force of air resistance. The forces are unbalanced and the skydiver accelerates.

The force of air resistance increases until it is equal to the skydiver's weight.

In the horizontal parts of the graph, the skydiver is travelling at terminal velocity. The force of air resistance is equal to the skydiver's weight. The forces are balanced and the skydiver travels at a constant velocity.

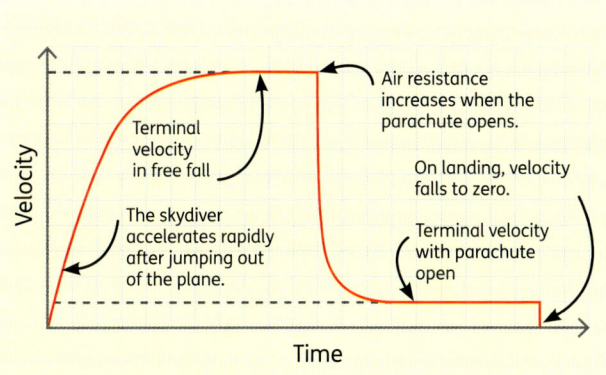

Question
A skydiver jumps out of a plane. After falling 151.25 m, they have reached terminal velocity.

Calculate the terminal velocity of the skydiver. Assume that their acceleration is 10 m/s².

Answer
Initial velocity = 0 m/s

(Final velocity)² − (Initial velocity)² = 2 × Acceleration × Distance

(Final velocity)² − (0)² = 2 × 10 × 151.25

(Final velocity)² = 3,025

Final velocity = √3,025

= 55 m/s

Newton's Laws of Motion

Key facts

- Newton's first law states that if the resultant force on an object is zero, it will keep moving at the same velocity or stay stationary.
- Newton's second law states that the acceleration of an object is proportional to the resultant force acting on the object and inversely proportional to the mass of the object.
- Newton's third law states that every force is accompanied by an equal force acting in the opposite direction.

Newton's first law

When the resultant force acting on an object is zero and the object is stationary, it remains stationary.

When the resultant force acting on an object is zero and the object is moving, it continues to move at the same velocity.

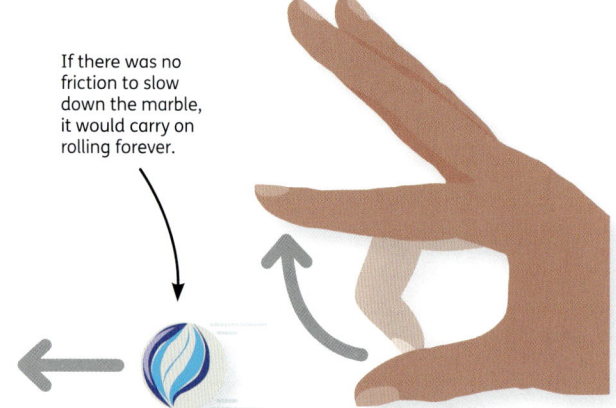

If there was no friction to slow down the marble, it would carry on rolling forever.

Newton's second law

Newton's second law can be written as an equation:

Resultant force (in N) = Mass (in kg) × Acceleration (in m/s²)

Question
The force provided by the engine of a car is 1,875 N. The mass of the car is 1,250 kg.

Calculate the acceleration of the car.

Answer
Rearrange the equation to make acceleration the subject:

$$\text{Acceleration} = \frac{\text{Force}}{\text{Mass}} = \frac{1{,}875}{1{,}250} = 1.5 \text{ m/s}^2$$

RAPPING UP!

Newton told me the first **law of motion**.
Now I'm gonna tell you his notion.
An object at **rest** stays frozen
Unless pushed on by something potent.

Second law's a little bit harder.
With more **force** it accelerates faster.
Third one comes with this caption:
Every action must have a **reaction**.

This applies to Lambos and Porsches.
Hardest of all of these courses.
They divide up into two sources:
Contact and non-contact forces.

Reaction, tension in this instance,
Then friction and air resistance.
Magnetic and gravitation,
Electrostatic is a sensation.

Forces

Exam tip

- Action-reaction forces act on difference objects.
- Balanced forces act on the same object.

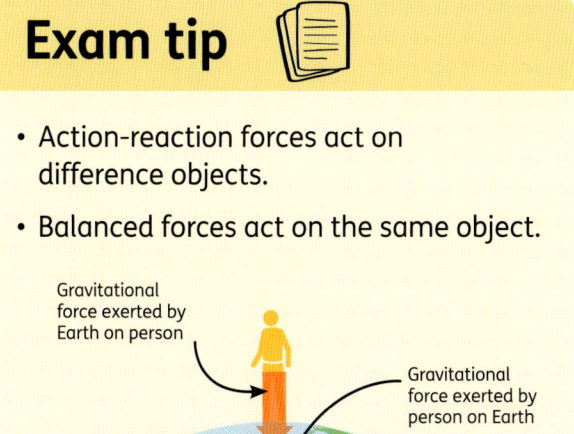

Newton's third law

Whenever two objects interact, the forces they exert on each other are equal and opposite. Every force has an equal and opposite reaction force. These are known as action-reaction forces.

Pairs of action and reaction forces are always the same type of force and act between pairs of objects.

For example, a person leaning against a wall exerts a force against the wall. The wall exerts an equal and opposite force on the person.

Science skills

Investigating acceleration

You can use the equipment shown in the diagram to investigate the effects of force and mass on acceleration. The slope of the ramp compensates for friction. The angle should be adjusted so that the trolley with no masses on it rolls at a constant speed when you give it a gentle push.

To investigate the effect of mass, vary the number of masses on the trolley.

To investigate the effect of force, vary the number of masses on the hanger.

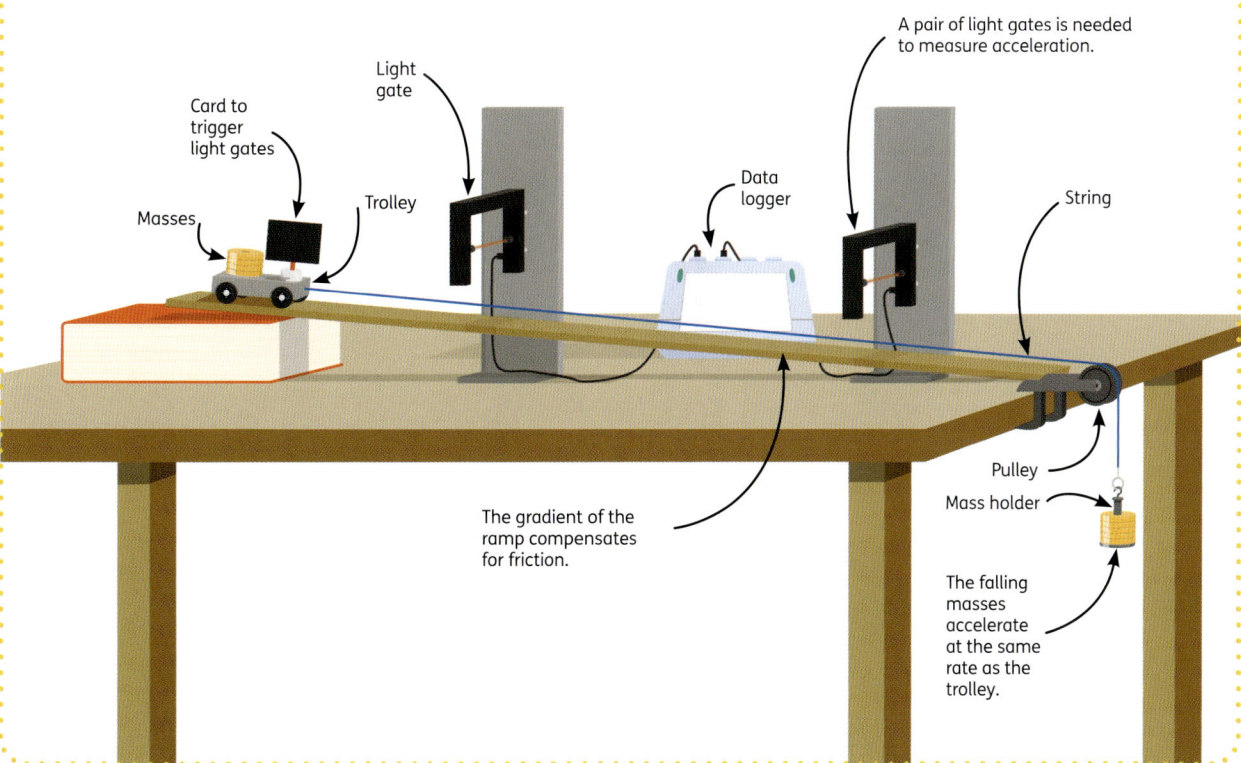

Forces and Braking

Key facts

- Stopping distance = Thinking distance + Braking distance
- A driver's reaction time can be affected by tiredness, drugs and alcohol.
- Human reaction time is in the range 0.2–0.9 seconds.

Stopping distance

The **stopping distance** of a vehicle is the sum of the distance the vehicle travels during the driver's **reaction time** (**thinking distance**) and the distance it travels under the braking force (**braking distance**).

The reaction time is the time between a person detecting a stimulus (such as seeing a hazard on the road) and their response (such as pressing the brake pedal).

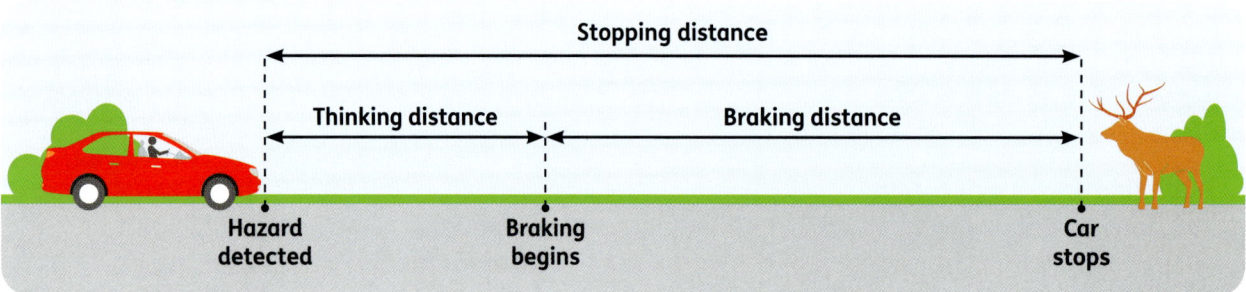

For a given braking force:
- The greater the speed of the vehicle, the greater the stopping distance.
- The greater the mass of the vehicle, the greater the stopping distance.

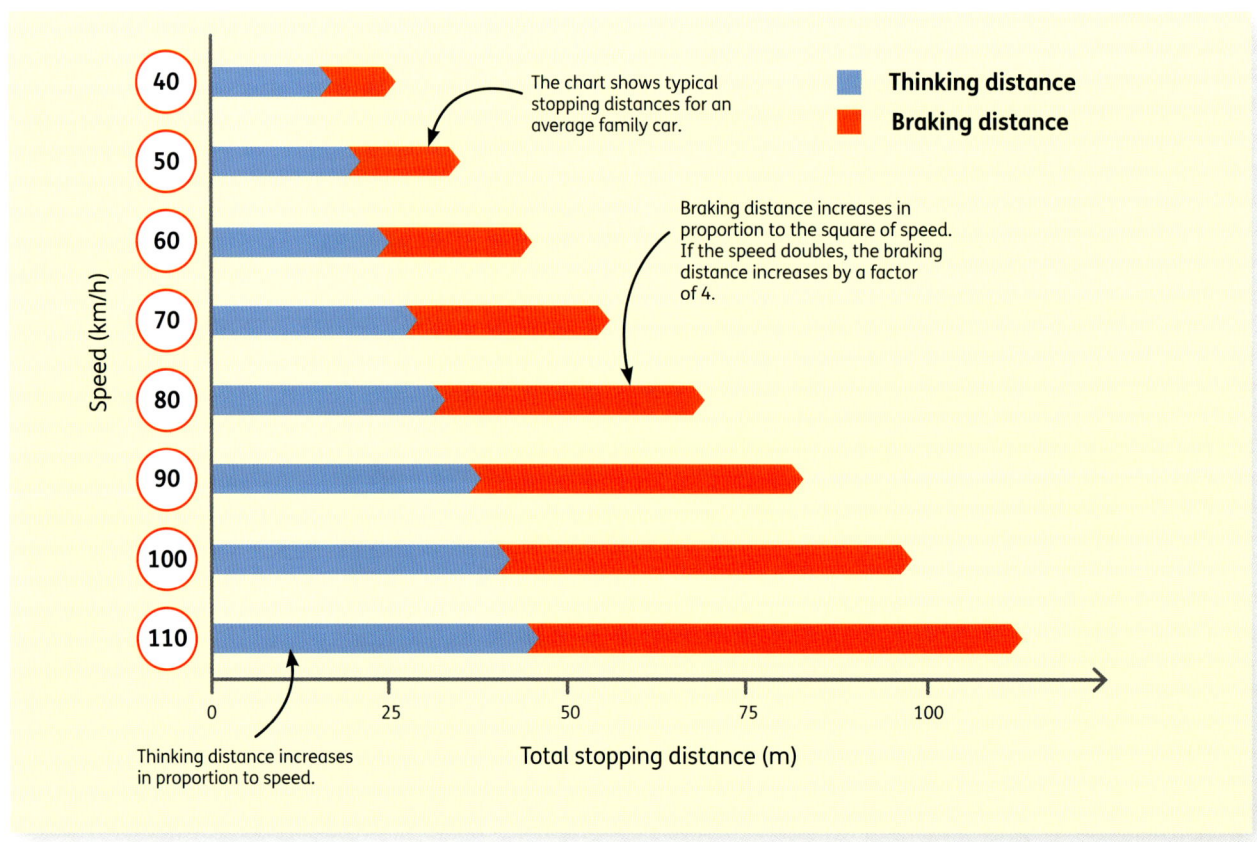

The chart shows typical stopping distances for an average family car.

Braking distance increases in proportion to the square of speed. If the speed doubles, the braking distance increases by a factor of 4.

Thinking distance increases in proportion to speed.

Forces

Reaction time

Reaction times vary from person to person. Typical values range from 0.2 s to 0.9 s.

Factors affecting reaction time

A driver's reaction time can be affected by different factors. Most drivers take about 0.7 seconds to react to a hazard. However, this time can be increased more than three-fold (to above 2.1 seconds) if the driver has been drinking alcohol, taken any kind of medication, or distracted by a mobile phone. Reaction times can also be affected by tiredness. This is why you see signs on long distance roads suggesting drivers take a break.

Science skills

Measuring reaction time

- One person holds a ruler just above a second person's hand. The zero on the scale should be by the second person's hand.
- The first person drops the ruler without warning and the second person tries to catch the ruler.
- The distance that the ruler drops can be used to calculate the reaction time.

Repeat with different circumstances. For example:

- The person is having a conversation with another person.
- The person is listening to music on headphones.
- The light conditions in the room are darkened.

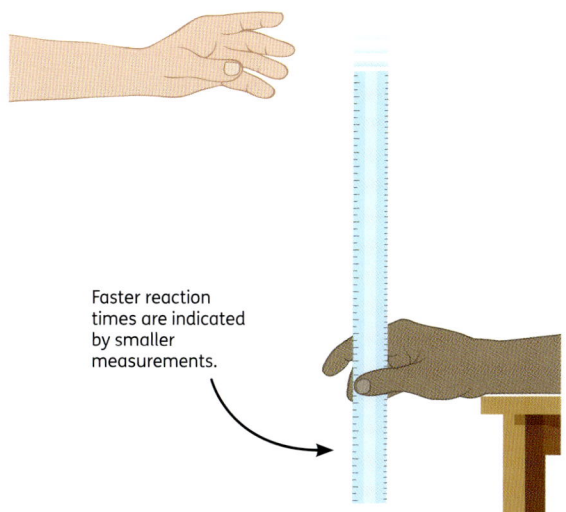

Faster reaction times are indicated by smaller measurements.

Distance ruler dropped (m)	Reaction time (s)
0.1	0.14
0.2	0.20
0.3	0.25
0.4	0.29
0.5	0.32
0.6	0.35
0.7	0.38
0.8	0.40
0.9	0.43

Other methods

You can also use devices where a light comes on randomly. You press a button when you see the light come on. The device provides a direct measurement of reaction time.

Braking Distance

Key facts

- Braking distance can be affected by various factors: road conditions, condition of the brakes, condition of the tyres.
- The braking distance required to stop a car safely increases in proportion to the square of the car's speed.
- The momentum of a vehicle can be calculated using the equation

  Momentum = Mass × Velocity

- The force acting on a vehicle can be calculated using the equation

  $$\text{Force} = \frac{\text{Change in momentum}}{\text{Time}}$$

Factors affecting braking distance

- Road conditions. If the road surface is wet or icy, this can reduce friction between the road and the tyres. The stopping force is smaller, so braking distance increases. It can also cause skids.
- Condition of the brakes. If the brakes are worn or in poor condition, then the friction between the brakes and the wheels is reduced. The stopping force is smaller, so braking distance increases.
- Condition of the tyres. If the tyres are worn or in poor condition, the friction between the road and the tyres is reduced. The stopping force is smaller so braking distance increases.

Braking distance and energy

When the brakes are used to slow down the car, they exert a force and do work. The work done braking is equal to the change in kinetic energy.

We can combine the equation for work done with the equation for kinetic energy to make a new equation.

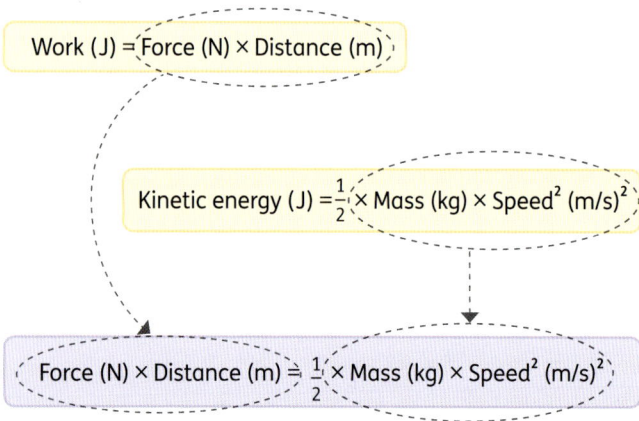

Work done by brakes

When a force is applied to the brakes of a vehicle, work is done by the friction force between the brakes and the wheels. Energy is transferred from the kinetic energy store of the car to the thermal energy store of the brakes. The temperature of the brakes increases.

Speed and safety

The greater the speed of a vehicle, the greater the braking force needed to stop the vehicle in a certain distance.

When the speed doubles, the braking distance is four times greater. When the speed is tripled, the braking distance is nine times greater.

Braking force and safety

The greater the braking force, the greater the deceleration of the vehicle. When the deceleration is large, the brakes can overheat and the driver may lose control of the vehicle.

Momentum and safety

We can work out the momentum of a vehicle using the equation:

Momentum = Mass × Velocity

When a vehicle slows down, its momentum changes and we can work out the force acting on the vehicle as it slows down using the equation

$$\text{Force} = \frac{\text{Change in momentum}}{\text{Time}}$$

Safety features in vehicles, such as seat belts, crumple zones and air bags, are designed to increase the time over which a change in momentum happens, therefore reducing the force on the car (and its occupants). A crash test checks that these features work as intended.

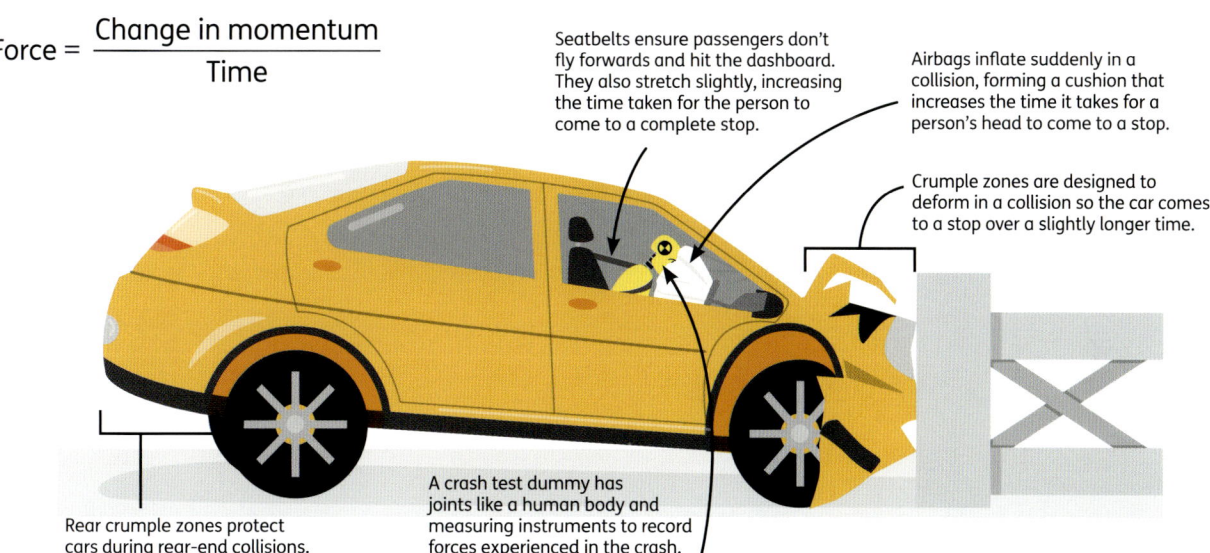

Seatbelts ensure passengers don't fly forwards and hit the dashboard. They also stretch slightly, increasing the time taken for the person to come to a complete stop.

Airbags inflate suddenly in a collision, forming a cushion that increases the time it takes for a person's head to come to a stop.

Crumple zones are designed to deform in a collision so the car comes to a stop over a slightly longer time.

A crash test dummy has joints like a human body and measuring instruments to record forces experienced in the crash.

Rear crumple zones protect cars during rear-end collisions.

Question
A car with a mass of 1,100 kg travels at about 50 km/h (14 m/s). The driver approaches some traffic lights and brakes for 20 seconds. The car stops. Calculate the force acting on the car.

14 m/s   0 m/s

Answer
Momentum at start:
1,100 kg × 14 m/s = 15,400 kgm/s

Momentum at end:
1,100 kg × 0 m/s = 0 kgm/s

Change in momentum:
= 0 kgm/s − 15,400 kgm/s
= −15,400 kgm/s

$$\text{Force} = \frac{-15,400}{0.05}$$

= 770 N

Question
A uniform braking force of 2,000 N is applied to the wheels of a 1,200 kg car travelling at 15 m/s (about 54 km/h).

a) What is its braking distance?

b) What would the braking distance be at twice that speed?

Answer
a) Rearrange the equation to make distance the subject.

$$\text{Distance} = \frac{\text{Mass} \times \text{Speed}^2}{2 \times \text{Force}}$$

$$= \frac{1,200 \times 15^2}{2 \times 2,000}$$

= 67.5 m

b) Twice the speed = 15 × 2 = 30 m/s

$$\text{Distance} = \frac{1,200 \times 30^2}{2 \times 2,000}$$

= 270 m

Brain Booster

Forces
Recap Quiz

 Find a pen and paper and work through these revision questions.

1. Explain the difference between a scalar and a vector.

2. One person pushes a piano with a force of 100 N, but another person pushes back the opposite way with a force of 150 N. What is the resultant force?

3. A person pushes a box 8 m. The force applied by the person is 50 N. Calculate the work done on the box.

4. A person has a mass of 75 kg. Calculate the weight of the person on Earth. Assume that the gravitational field strength is 9.8 N/kg.

5. Explain the difference between elastic deformation and inelastic deformation.

6. Explain why atmospheric pressure varies with height above the surface of the Earth.

7. Explain how to find speed from a distance–time graph.

8. What does a horizontal line on a velocity–time graph represent?

9. A train accelerates from 10 m/s to 40 m/s in 40 s. Calculate a the acceleration of the train.

10. A car is moving at a constant velocity and the resultant force on it is zero. Explain what happens in terms of Newton's first law of motion.

11. A person is sitting on a chair. Identify the Newton's third law pairs of forces acting on the person and the chair.

12. Explain what is meant by stopping distance.

13. Give **three** factors that can affect a person's reaction time.

Check your answers on page **109-110**.

Waves

At the end of this chapter, you should be able to:

- ✓ Explain what transverse and longitudinal waves are.
- ✓ Describe the properties of waves.
- ✓ Calculate wave speed, frequency and wavelength.
- ✓ Measure the speed of sound in air and measure the speed of ripples on water.
- ✓ Draw a ray diagram to show reflection of a wave at a surface.
- ✓ Describe how waves can be reflected, transmitted or absorbed at the boundary between two materials.
- ✓ Describe the different parts of the electromagnetic spectrum.
- ✓ Describe the uses of different parts of the electromagnetic spectrum.
- ✓ Explain the hazards of high-energy electromagnetic radiation.
- ✓ Construct ray diagrams for converging/convex and diverging/concave lenses.
- ✓ Explain how the colour of an object is determined by the wavelengths of light that are reflected.
- ✓ Explain that the colour of a filter is determined by the wavelengths of light that are transmitted.

Properties of Waves

Key facts

- Transverse waves can travel through a medium and a vacuum.
- Longitudinal waves need a medium to travel through, such as air or water. They cannot travel in a vacuum.
- Wave speed (in m/s) = Frequency (in Hz) × Wavelength (in m)
- Period (in s) = $\dfrac{1}{\text{Frequency (in Hz)}}$

Properties of waves

Long wavelength, low frequency

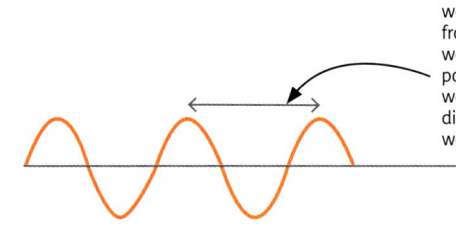

The **wavelength** of a wave is the distance from a point on one wave to the equivalent point on the adjacent wave. Here it is the distance from one wave peak to the next.

Short wavelength, high frequency

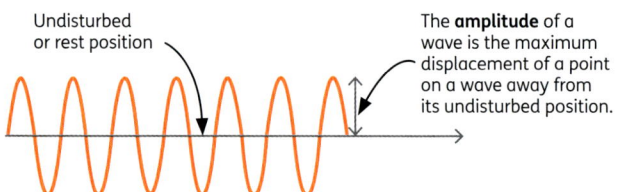

Undisturbed or rest position

The **amplitude** of a wave is the maximum displacement of a point on a wave away from its undisturbed position.

The **frequency** of a wave is the number of waves passing a point each second.

The **wave speed** is the speed at which the wave moves (or energy is transferred) through the medium.

Transverse waves
A water wave is a transverse wave.

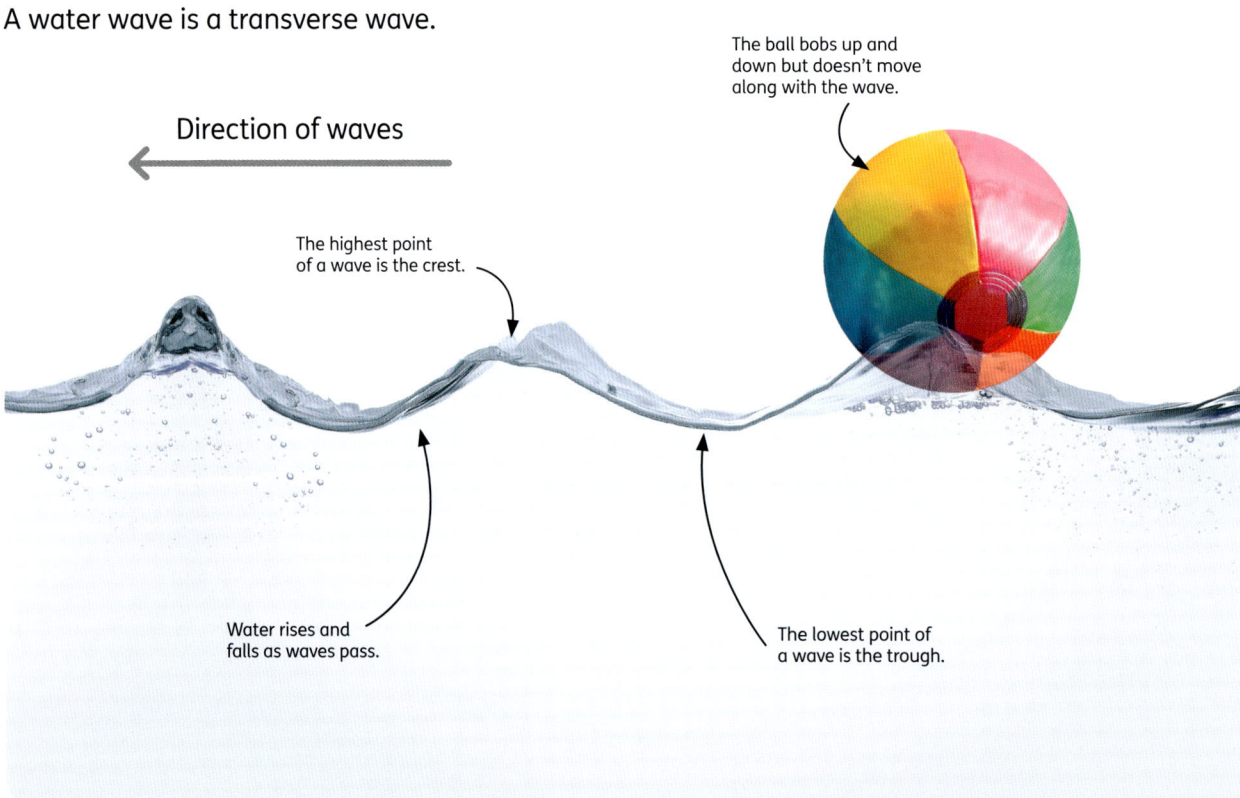

Direction of waves

The ball bobs up and down but doesn't move along with the wave.

The highest point of a wave is the crest.

Water rises and falls as waves pass.

The lowest point of a wave is the trough.

Longitudinal waves

A sound wave is a longitudinal wave.

Compression, where the air particles are squeezed together

Rarefaction, where the air particles are further apart

Direction of travel

Vibration of particles forwards and backwards along the direction of travel of the wave. The particles don't move along with the wave.

Wavelength

Wave calculations

Question
A sound has a frequency of 100 Hz. What is the period of the sound?

Answer
$$\text{Period} = \frac{1}{\text{Frequency}}$$
$$= \frac{1}{100}$$
$$= 0.01 \text{ s}$$

Question
In a ripple tank, five waves pass a point each second. The wavelength of the waves is 6 cm. Calculate the wave speed in metres per second.

Answer
Wavelength = 6 cm = 0.06 m

Wave speed = Frequency × Wavelength
$$= 5 \times 0.06$$
$$= 0.3 \text{ m/s}$$

RAPPING UP!

This is a wave.
It **os-ci-lates**.
That just means it vibrates.
Check its shape.
Amplitude is in this place
but wavelength goes this way.

Hz, Hz – that's the unit for **frequency**.
Counts the waves that pass this point you can see per secs.

This wave we call trans-
verse – it goes **up and down** in my hand.
One more wave's longitutinal.
This goes **side to side** in this coil.

Let's take a look at the science.
Oscillation and direction.
Compare how they are aligning.
Transverse is not in alignment.
You know this is a right angle.
Cuts through the line like Play-Doh.
Unlike longitudinal, waves that
are parallel.

Measuring the Speed of Waves

Key facts

- You can use a ripple tank to measure the speed of ripples on a water surface.
- You can measure the speed of sound in air by timing how long it takes a sound to reach a person.
- Sonar relies on measuring how long it takes for a sound to be reflected by an object and return to the ship.

Changes in velocity, frequency and wavelength

The speed of sound is different in different materials. As wave speed, frequency and wavelength are related by the wave equation, when the wave speed changes, the other two variables should change.

The frequency of a sound does not change. When sound enters a different material, the wavelength changes along with the wave speed.

Science skills

Measuring the speed of ripples on the surface of water

- Use the equipment shown in the diagram.
- Take a photo of the shadow of the ripples on the paper and the ruler. Work out the wavelength.
- Measure how many waves pass a point on the paper in 10 seconds. Divide this by 10 to work out the frequency.
- Use the wave speed equation to calculate the speed of the ripples.

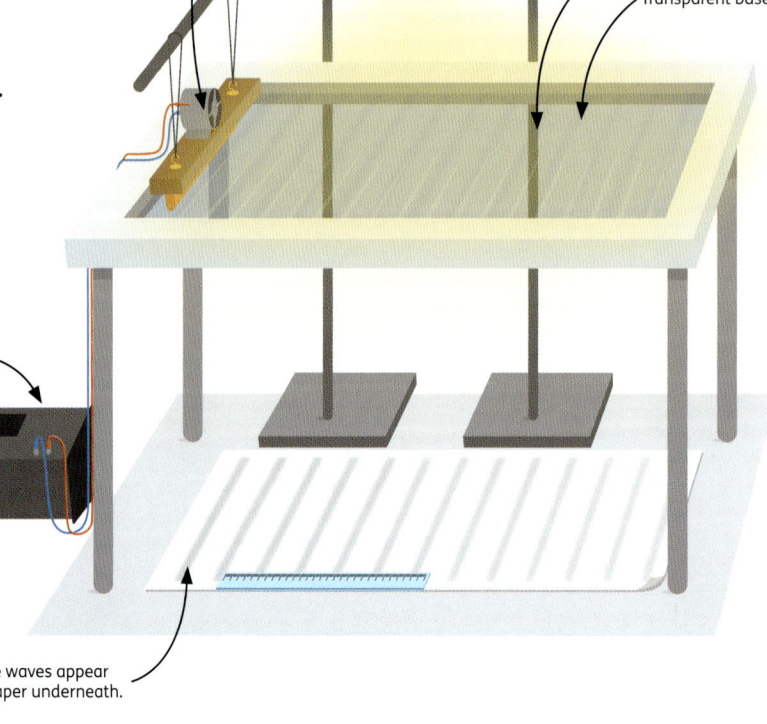

A motor moves the paddle up and down, creating waves.

Lamp

Water

Transparent base

Changing the voltage from the power supply changes the frequency.

Shadows of the waves appear on the white paper underneath.

Waves

Science skills

Measuring the speed of sound waves in air

- When the first person hits the cymbals, the second person starts the stopwatch.
- When the second person hears the cymbals they stop the stopwatch.
- The equation Speed = Distance ÷ Time is used to work out the speed of sound in air.

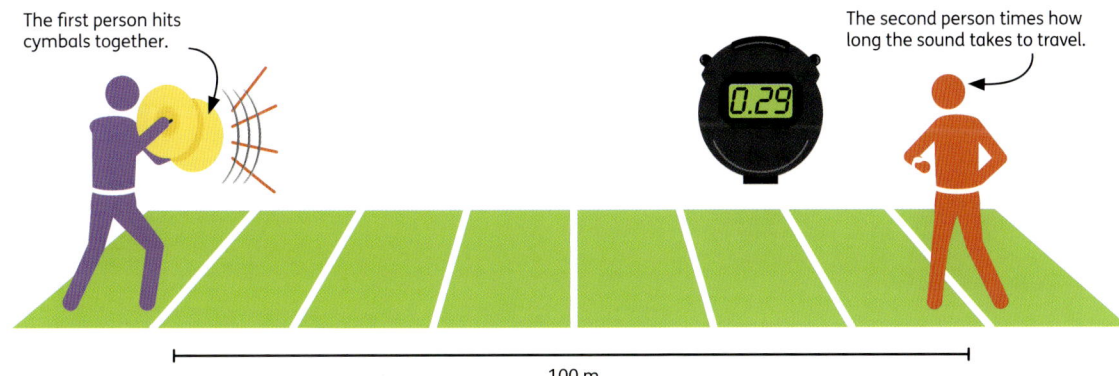

Measuring the speed of sound waves in a solid

- Strike the bar with a hammer. Use a smartphone app to measure the frequency of the loudest sound detected when the phone is next to the bar.
- The wavelength of the loudest sound is twice the length of the bar.
- Use the wave speed equation to calculate the speed of sound.

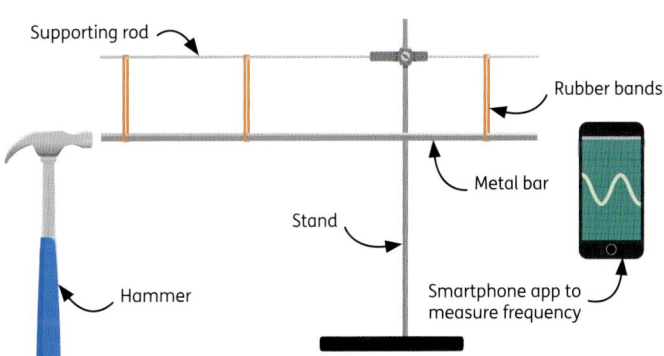

Sonar

The diagram shows how sonar is used to locate shoals of fish or map the seabed.

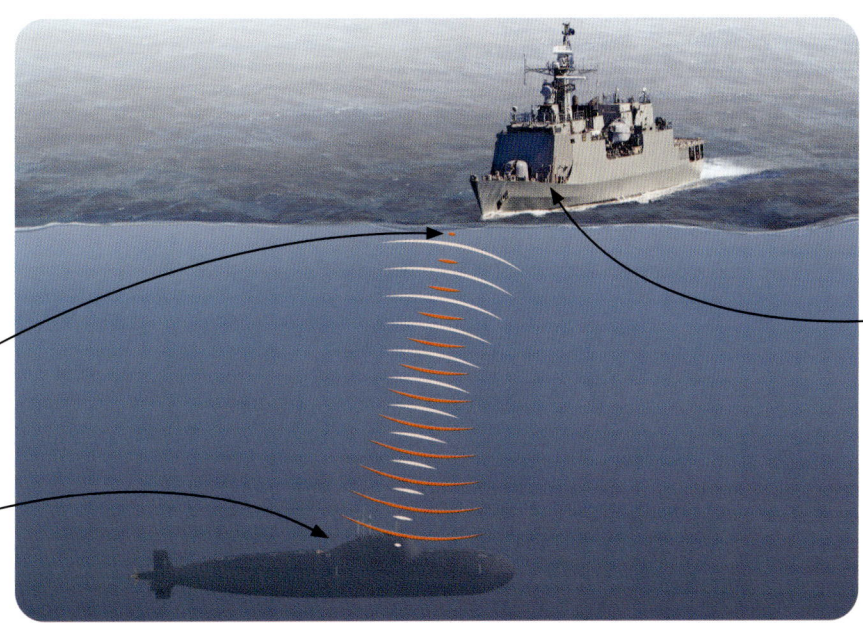

1. Pulses of ultrasound are emitted by a transmitter.
2. Objects underwater reflect the sound waves.
3. A receiver on the ship detects the echoes and calculates the object's distance.

Waves

Reflection and Refraction

Key facts

- When light is reflected by a mirror or waves are reflected from a barrier, the **angle of incidence** equals the **angle of reflection**.
- **Refraction** is the change in direction when a wave passes from one medium to another.

Science skills

Investigating reflection

- You can use the equipment in the image to investigate reflection from a mirror.
- Draw two perpendicular lines on the paper. Position the mirror on the horizontal line, as shown. The vertical line represents the normal.
- Shine a ray of light at the mirror. Trace the light ray. Then use a protractor to measure the angles of incidence and reflection.
- Repeat with the light ray at different angles to the mirror.
- You could also use a ripple tank. Put a straight barrier at different angles to the waves and observe what happens.
- In both cases, Angle of incidence = Angle of reflection.

angle of incidence = angle of reflection

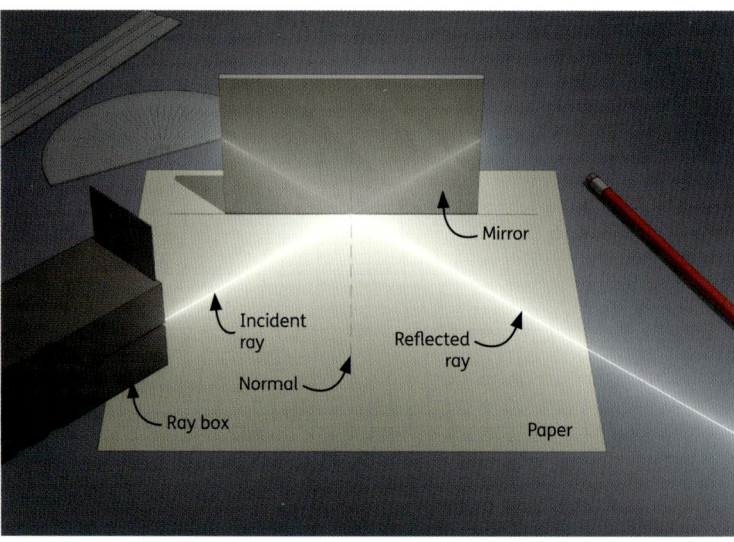

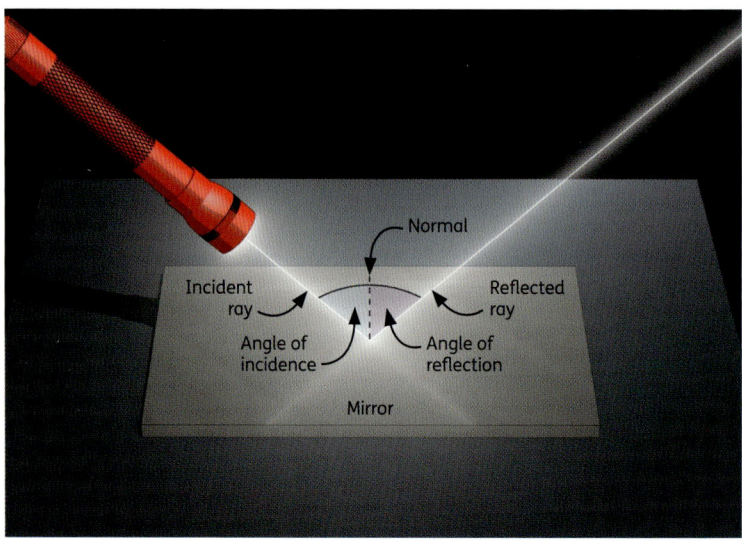

Waves

Image in a mirror

The image shows a ray diagram of how an image is formed in a mirror.

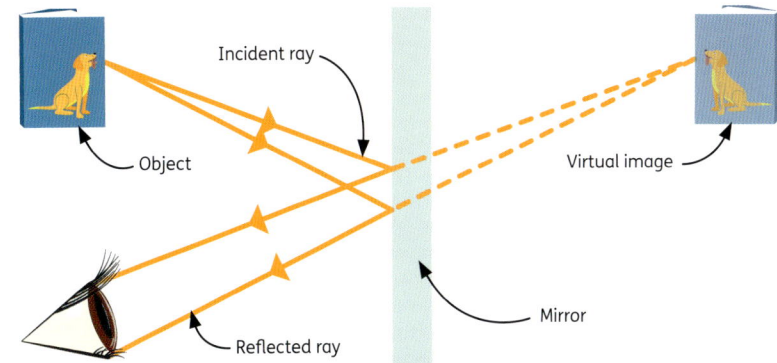

Science skills

Investigating refraction

- You can use the equipment shown in the diagram to investigate how the angle of refraction varies with the angle of incidence.
- Use a pencil to mark the path of the ray with small crosses, including where the ray enters and leaves the glass block.
- Remove the block and draw straight lines connecting the crosses. Measure the angles of incidence and refraction.
- Light bends towards the normal when it passes from air to glass.
- Light bends away from the normal when it passes from glass to air.
- The incident ray and emerging ray are parallel.

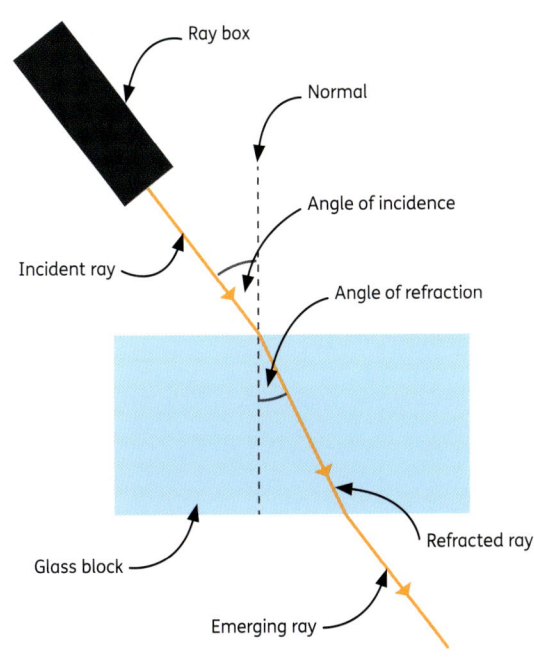

RAPPING UP!

Today's class is looking at **light**.
It's a wave on the EM spectrum.
It's a **wave** we see with our eyes.
Let's explore both reflect and refraction.

I want you to know those perfect.
The first word up is "**reflect**".
Light bounces up at the surface,
Exactly how you'd expect.

The second word here's "**refract**".
The light ray enters this block.
Where the light ray touches the boundary
It changes direction – it doesn't stop.

The glass is denser than air
So the **light bends** towards the normal.
When it reaches over there
It bends away – now let's make it formal.

Now students are teaching me.
I've learned new slang, I'm proud to **admit**.
Now I understand what they mean
When they tell me my classes are lit.

Electromagnetic Waves

Key facts

- **Electromagnetic waves** are transverse waves that transfer energy.
- Electromagnetic waves form a continuous **spectrum**.
- All types of electromagnetic wave travel at the same velocity through a vacuum (space) or air.

Electromagnetic waves

Energy is transferred when electromagnetic waves are emitted from one atom and absorbed by another. They range from radio waves with wavelengths of up to thousands of kilometres, to gamma rays with wavelengths of 3×10^{-12} metres.

The lower the wavelength, the higher the frequency and the greater the amount of energy transferred by the wave.

Visible light transfers energy from the Sun to the Earth.

They all travel at about 3×10^8 m/s (300,000 km/s) through a vacuum or through air.

Our eyes only see a limited range of electromagnetic waves in the region of visible light.

Electromagnetic spectrum

Generating electromagnetic waves
Electromagnetic waves can be generated or absorbed when there are changes in atoms and the nuclei of atoms. The waves have a wide frequency range.

Gamma rays originate from changes in the nucleus of an atom.

Visible light is emitted when electrons move from higher energy levels to lower energy levels. Electrons can move to higher energy levels when they absorb visible light.

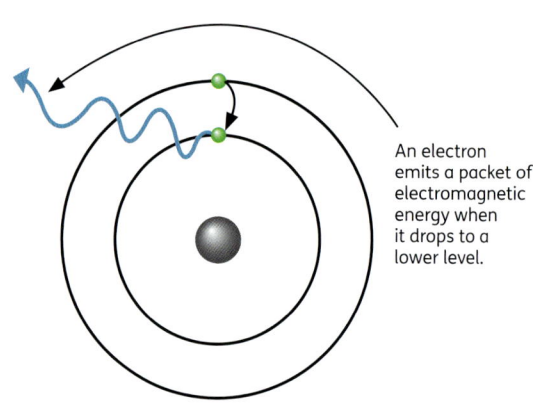

An electron emits a packet of electromagnetic energy when it drops to a lower level.

Oxygen atom

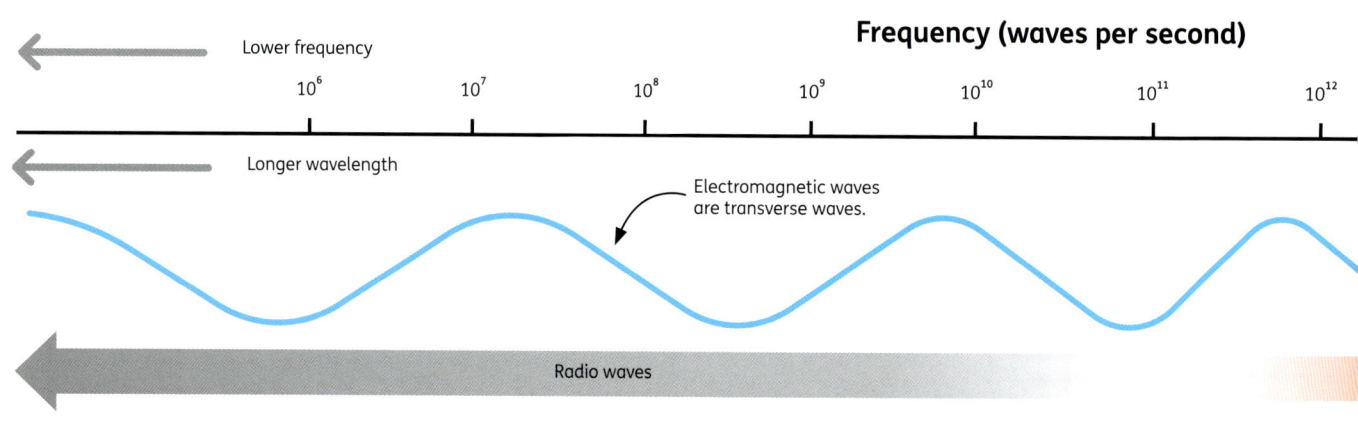

Waves

RAPPING UP!

This is electro mag spec.
Radio, micro and infrared.
Visible, ultraviolet and X.
Gamma rays last – it ain't that complex.

The longest **wavelength** is radio.
First one down, but still we got way to go.
Microwaves next for phone calls and **heating**.
Infrared's in the **remote** for the TV.

Visible light's in the middle of this chain.
Richard of York
Gave Belligerence In Vain.
UV light can be used when alone,
And **X-rays** we use to check up on bone.

Science skills

Investigating infrared radiation

You can investigate how the amount of infrared radiation radiated by a surface depends on the nature of that surface.

You measure the temperature of three cans that contain hot water over a fixed period of time.

The first can has a matt black outer surface, the second can has a white outer surface and the third has a shiny silver surface.

You should find that the matt black can cools down the quickest, then the white can. The silver can cools down the slowest.

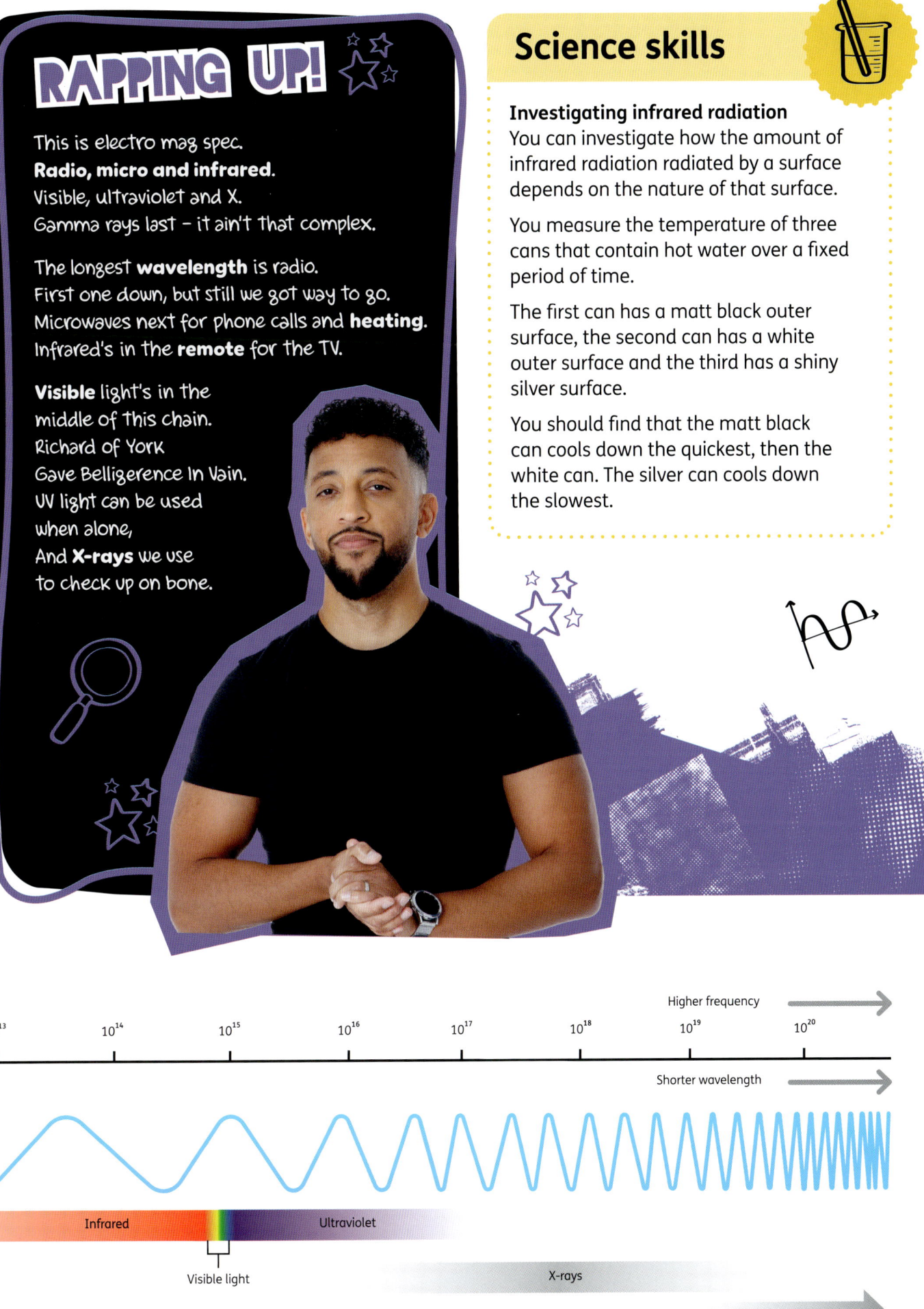

Uses, Hazards and Visible Light

Key facts

- Each part of the electromagnetic spectrum has its uses.
- Radio waves are produced by alternating electric currents.
- Radio waves induce alternating electric currents in antennae (aerials).
- The frequency of a radio wave is the same as the frequency of the alternating current that generated it.
- Higher energy electromagnetic waves can ionise atoms.
- **Specular reflection** occurs when light is reflected from a smooth surface in one direction.
- **Diffuse reflection** occurs when light is reflected from a rough surface in many directions.

Uses

Radio waves are used to transmit television and radio signals, as well as phone calls and internet data.

Microwaves are used for satellite communications and cooking food.

Infrared is used in electrical heaters, for cooking food, infrared cameras and sending signals from a TV remote control to the TV.

Visible light is used in fibreoptic communications. We also use this to illuminate our surroundings, as well as in TV and mobile phone screens.

Ultraviolet is used to kill bacteria and viruses and to detect forged banknotes. It can also be used to make fluorescent objects glow.

X-rays are used for medical imaging and to check contents of bags in airport security.

Gamma rays are used for cancer treatments and to sterilise medical equipment.

Radio communication

Radio frequencies used for communication (including television signals) vary from low frequencies (with wavelengths measured in kilometres) to high frequencies (with wavelengths measured in centimetres). High-frequency waves travel in straight lines and can be relayed using satellites. Lower frequency waves are reflected by the ionosphere (a layer of the Earth's atmosphere) and so they can travel beyond the horizon. The diagram shows how radio communication works.

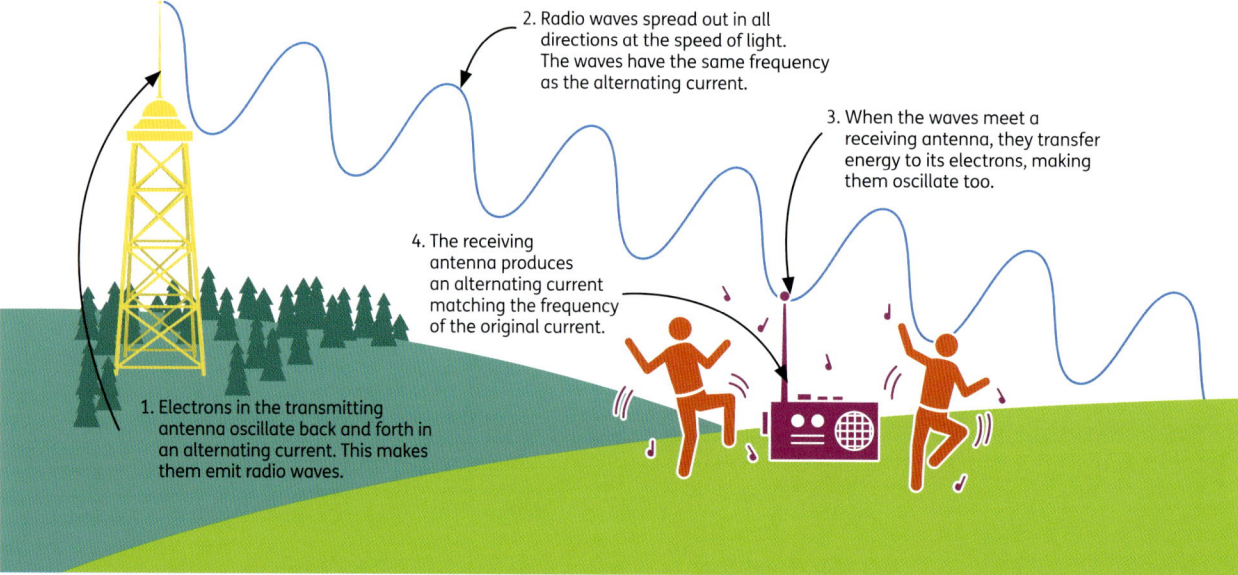

1. Electrons in the transmitting antenna oscillate back and forth in an alternating current. This makes them emit radio waves.
2. Radio waves spread out in all directions at the speed of light. The waves have the same frequency as the alternating current.
3. When the waves meet a receiving antenna, they transfer energy to its electrons, making them oscillate too.
4. The receiving antenna produces an alternating current matching the frequency of the original current.

Hazards

Higher energy electromagnetic waves can ionise atoms by removing electrons from them.

Ultraviolet radiation can harm skin cells, causing sunburn, and can cause skin to age prematurely. There is also an increased risk of cancer. It can also damage the retina of the human eye.

Both X-rays and gamma rays can penetrate the body and damage the DNA in cells. This can lead to mutations that cause cancer. The risk depends on the dose. Large doses of gamma rays can be fatal.

Radiation dose is a measure of the risk of harm resulting from exposure to the body. It is measured in sieverts.

Visible light

Each colour within the visible light spectrum has its own narrow band of wavelength and frequency.

The colour of an opaque object is determined by which wavelengths of light are more strongly reflected. Wavelengths that are not reflected are absorbed.

The red ball appears red because its surface absorbs all the wavelengths except red. Red light is reflected.

Infrared and black bodies

All objects (bodies), emit and absorb infrared radiation, at all temperatures. As temperature increases, the amount of infrared radiation an object radiates in a given time increases.

A perfect black body is an object that absorbs all of the radiation incident on it. A black body does not reflect or transmit any radiation. A good absorber is also a good emitter, so a perfect black body is also the best emitter.

The intensity and wavelength distribution of all radiation emitted by a body depends on the temperature of the body. The body emits radiation over a continuous range of wavelengths. The highest intensity is in the middle of the range.

The black ball appears black because all wavelengths are absorbed.

The white ball appears white because all wavelengths are reflected equally.

Transparent and translucent objects transmit light. You can see through a transparent object but not a translucent object.

Colour filters work by absorbing certain wavelengths and transmitting other wavelengths.

A red filter absorbs all colours apart from red light.

A green filter absorbs all colours apart from green light.

A blue filter absorbs all colours apart from blue light.

Waves

Lenses

Key facts

- A lens forms an image by refracting light.
- There are two types of lens: converging and diverging.
- Ray diagrams are used to show the formation of images by convex and concave lenses.
- Magnification = $\dfrac{\text{Image height}}{\text{Object height}}$

Exam tip

Always draw rays as straight lines. You should always use a ruler to draw them.

Lenses change the direction of light by refraction. Converging lenses bulge outwards in the middle. Diverging lenses are thinner in the middle.

Lenses

In a convex or converging lens, parallel rays of light are brought to a focus at the focal point. In a concave or diverging lens, parallel rays of light diverge or spread out and the focal point is where the rays appear to come from.

The distance from the lens to the focal point is called the focal length.

A more powerful lens is more curved and has a shorter focal length.

A **real image** can be projected onto a screen. A **virtual image** can only be seen by the person observing it.

Converging lens ray diagram
Draw three rays from the top of the object as shown in the diagram below. Draw one ray parallel with the axis to the lens and then through the focal point on the other side of the lens.

Draw a second ray through the middle of the lens. Draw a third ray through the focal point on the same side of the lens to the lens and then parallel to the axis.

The image is where the rays meet. The image is real, inverted (upside down) and diminished (smaller).

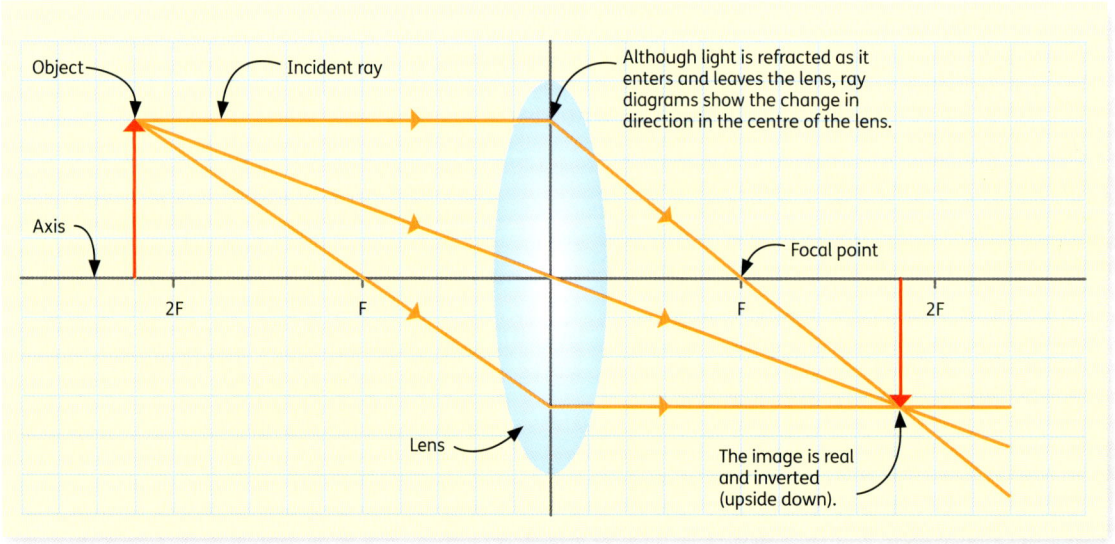

Magnifying glass
Draw two rays as shown and extend them to the left until they meet. The image is enlarged, upright, and virtual.

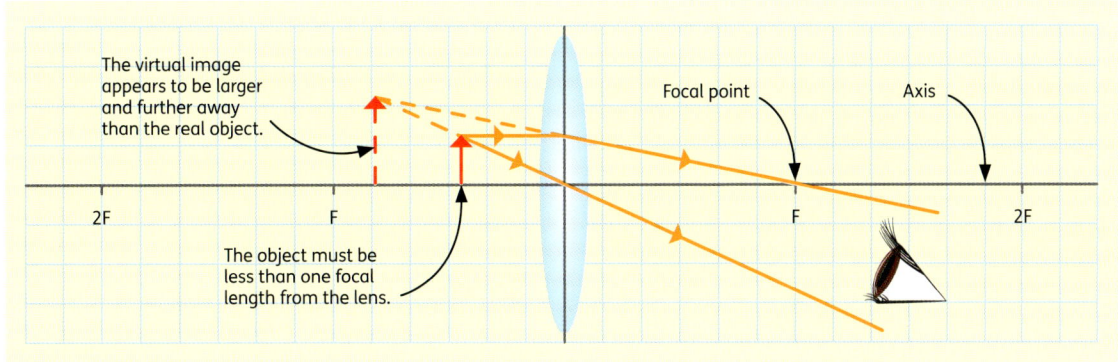

Diverging lens
Draw two rays as shown in the diagram. The image is virtual, upright and diminished.

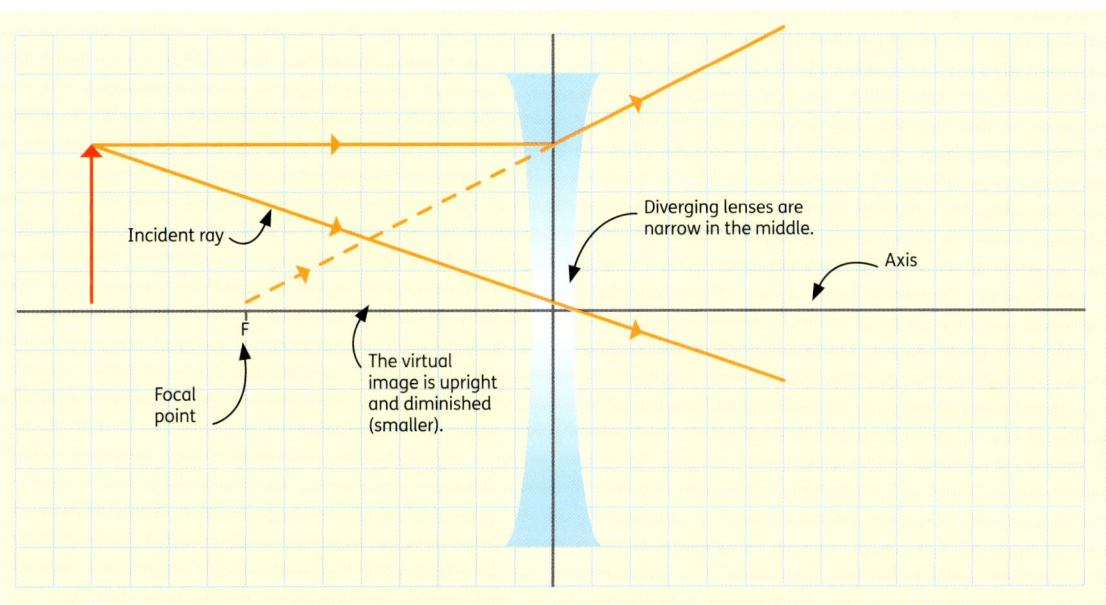

Calculating magnification

Magnification is a ratio, so the answer has no units.

Image height and object height must both be in the same units. Usually this will be millimetres or centimetres. Do not mix the units!

Question
An insect that is 8 mm long is viewed through a magnifying glass. The virtual image is 28 mm long. Calculate the magnification.

Answer
$$\text{Magnification} = \frac{\text{Image height}}{\text{Object height}}$$
$$= \frac{28}{8}$$
$$= 3.5$$

Question
A section of rock that is 10 mm long is viewed through a magnifying glass. The virtual image is 30 mm long. Calculate the magnification.

Answer
$$\text{Magnification} = \frac{\text{Image height}}{\text{Object height}}$$
$$= \frac{30}{10}$$
$$= 3$$

Waves Recap Quiz

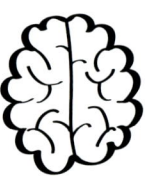

 Find a pen and paper and work through these revision questions.

1. Explain the difference between transverse and longitudinal waves.
2. Define the term "amplitude" as applied to a wave.
3. Waves are moving along a harbour wall and 8 waves pass a point in 5 seconds. The wavelength is 5 m. Calculate the speed of the waves.
4. Describe a method of measuring the speed of sound in air.
5. Describe what happens when an incident ray hits a glass block at an angle and passes through it.
6. What is an electromagnetic wave?
7. What type of surface is best at absorbing infrared radiation?
8. Give **three** uses of infrared radiation.
9. Describe the hazards of ultraviolet radiation.
10. Explain what colour a blue T-shirt will appear in green light.
11. Explain how a red filter produces red light.
12. Describe the image produced by a concave (diverging) lens.

Check your answers on pages **109-110**.

Magnetism and Electromagnetism

At the end of this chapter, you should be able to:

- ✓ Explain what a permanent magnet is.
- ✓ Explain how the poles of a magnet can attract or repel each other.
- ✓ Explain what an induced magnet is.
- ✓ Describe what a magnetic field is.
- ✓ Draw the magnetic field pattern of a bar magnet.
- ✓ Draw the magnetic field pattern around a current-carrying wire.
- ✓ Explain how a solenoid works.
- ✓ Interpret diagrams of electromagnetic devices.

Magnetism and Electromagnetism

Magnetism

Key facts

- A bar magnet is a permanent magnet, which means it is always magnetic.
- The metals iron, steel, nickel and cobalt are all magnetic.
- When two magnets are brought close together they exert a force on each other. This is a non-contact force.

Attraction and repulsion of magnets

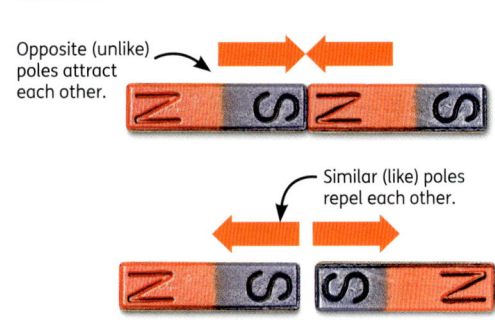

Opposite (unlike) poles attract each other.

Similar (like) poles repel each other.

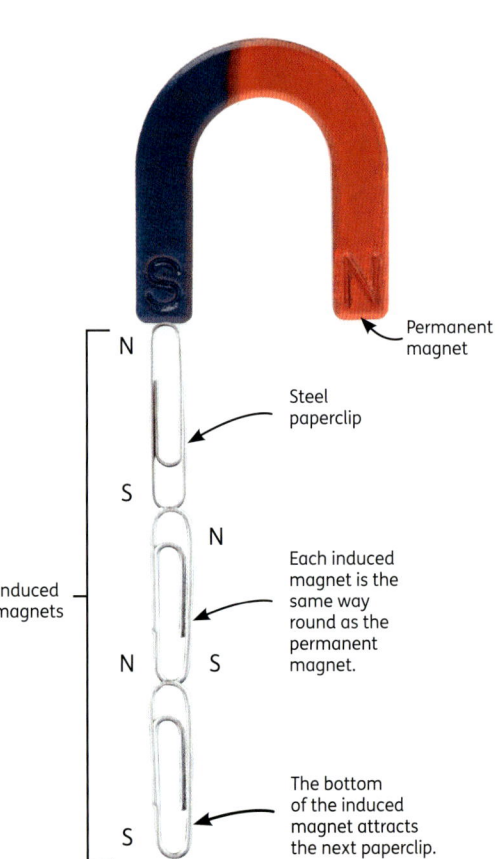

Permanent magnet

Steel paperclip

Induced magnets

Each induced magnet is the same way round as the permanent magnet.

The bottom of the induced magnet attracts the next paperclip.

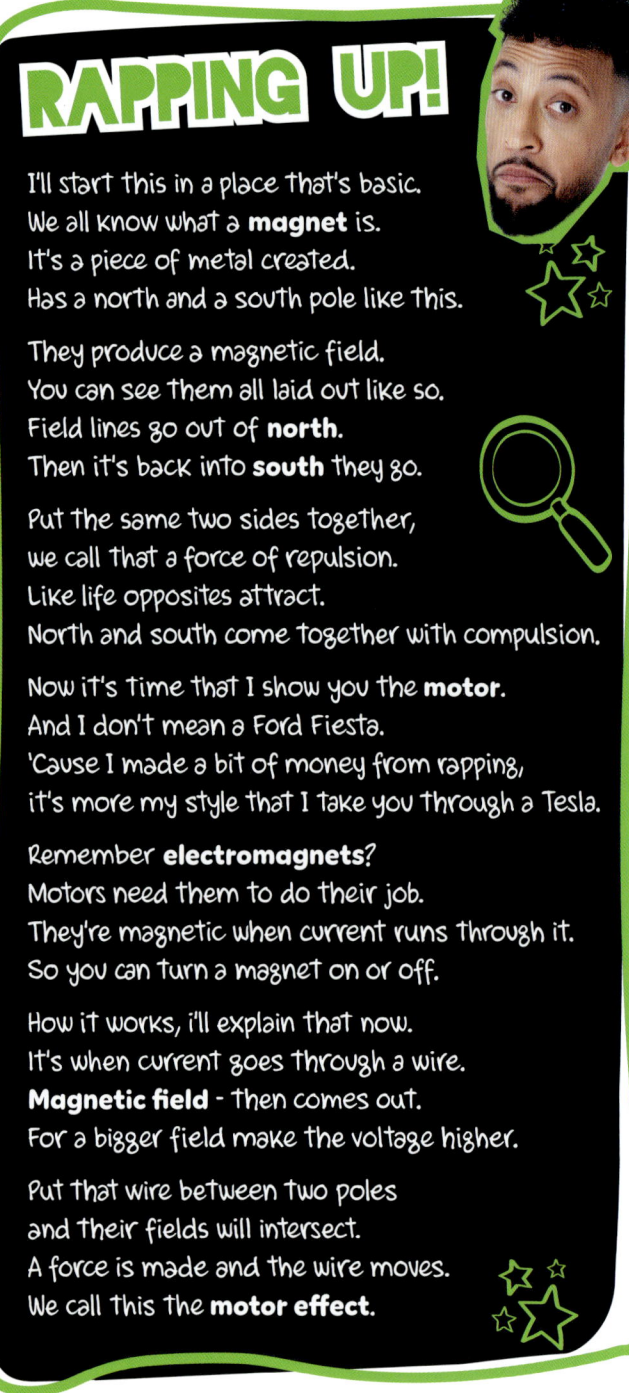

RAPPING UP!

I'll start this in a place that's basic.
We all know what a **magnet** is.
It's a piece of metal created.
Has a north and a south pole like this.

They produce a magnetic field.
You can see them all laid out like so.
Field lines go out of **north**.
Then it's back into **south** they go.

Put the same two sides together,
we call that a force of repulsion.
Like life opposites attract.
North and south come together with compulsion.

Now it's time that I show you the **motor**.
And I don't mean a Ford Fiesta.
'Cause I made a bit of money from rapping,
it's more my style that I take you through a Tesla.

Remember **electromagnets**?
Motors need them to do their job.
They're magnetic when current runs through it.
So you can turn a magnet on or off.

How it works, i'll explain that now.
It's when current goes through a wire.
Magnetic field - then comes out.
For a bigger field make the voltage higher.

Put that wire between two poles
and their fields will intersect.
A force is made and the wire moves.
We call this the **motor effect**.

Permanent and induced magnets

A permanent magnet produces its own magnetic field. An induced magnet is a material that becomes a magnet when it is placed in a magnetic field. Induced magnetism always causes a force of attraction.
When an induced magnet is removed from the magnetic field, it loses most of its magnetism quickly.

Magnetism and Electromagnetism

Magnetic fields

The region around a magnet where a force acts on another magnet or on a magnetic material is called the magnetic field.

A magnetic compass contains a small bar magnet. The Earth has a magnetic field. The compass needle points in the direction of the Earth's magnetic field.

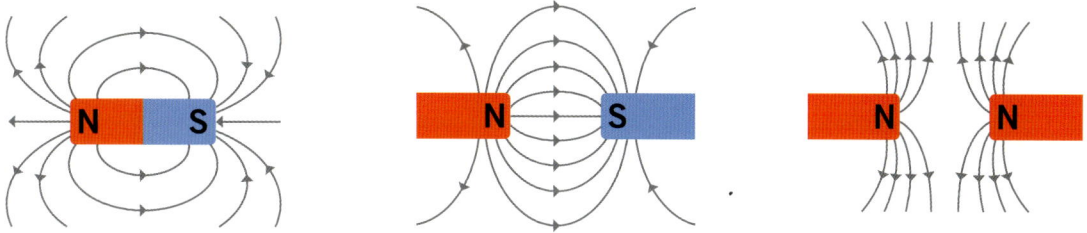

Field lines around a bar magnet, between opposite poles and between like poles.

Science skills

Plotting a magnetic field
You can use a plotting compass to draw the shape of a magnetic field.

Place the plotting compass near the north pole of the magnet.

Draw a dot at the end of the needle away from the magnet.

Move the plotting compass so that the other end of the needle is where you drew the dot.

Repeat until the plotting compass is at the other pole of the magnet.

Draw a smooth curve to connect all your dots. Repeat for other starting points at the pole of the magnet.

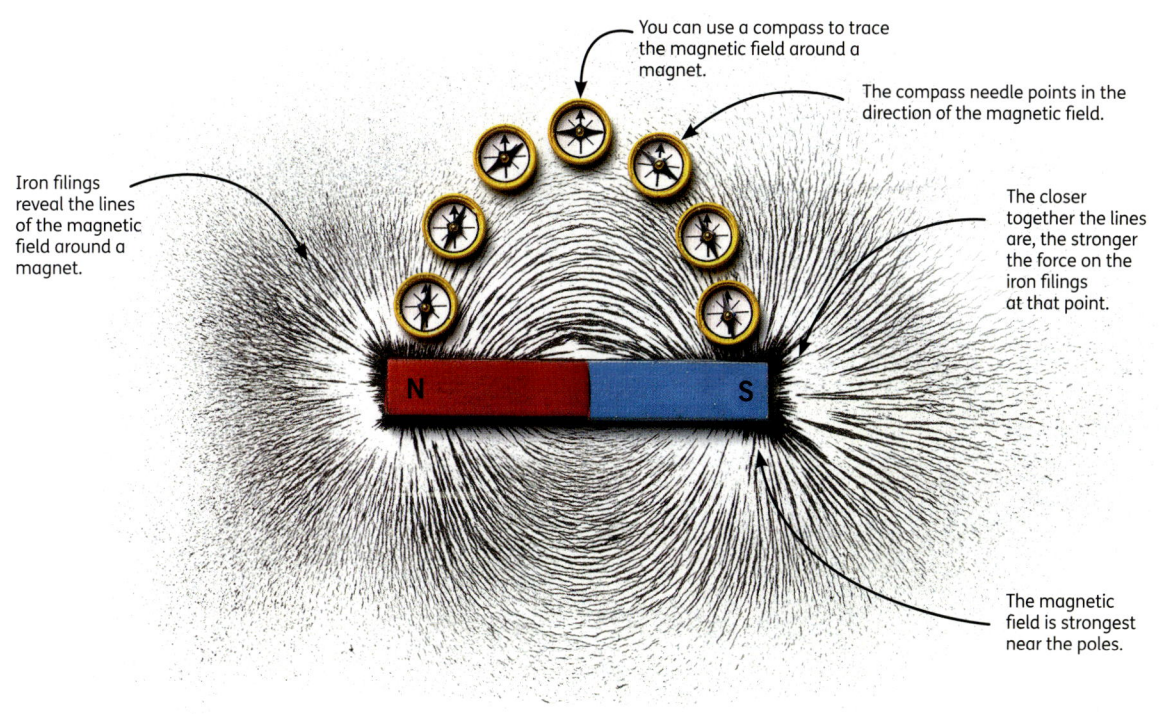

You can use a compass to trace the magnetic field around a magnet.

The compass needle points in the direction of the magnetic field.

Iron filings reveal the lines of the magnetic field around a magnet.

The closer together the lines are, the stronger the force on the iron filings at that point.

The magnetic field is strongest near the poles.

Electromagnetism

Key facts

- When a current flows through a wire, it creates a circular magnetic field around the wire.
- The right-hand grip rule shows the direction of the magnetic field produced when a current flows through a wire.
- A solenoid is a coil of wire with a current flowing through it.
- An iron core inside a solenoid strengthen the field of the electromagnet.
- Electromagnets are used in many devices, including relays.

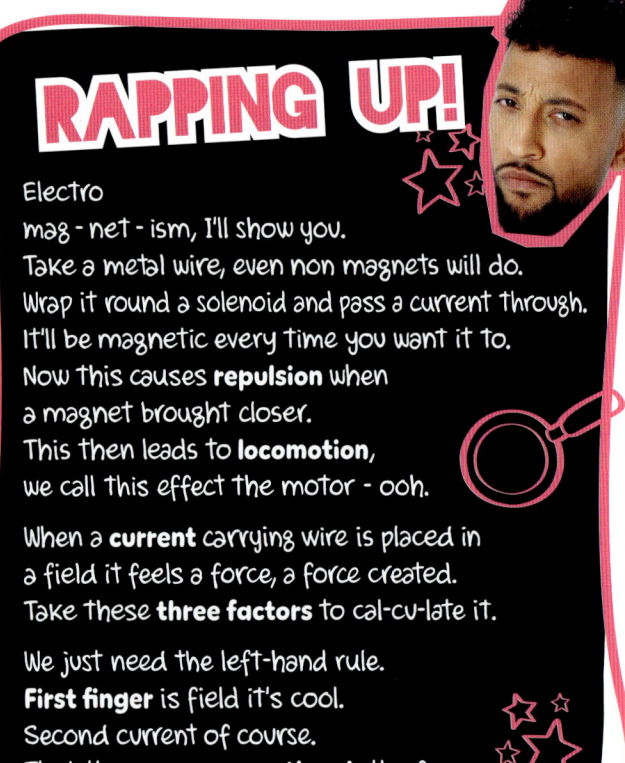

RAPPING UP!

Electro
mag - net - ism, I'll show you.
Take a metal wire, even non magnets will do.
Wrap it round a solenoid and pass a current through.
It'll be magnetic every time you want it to.
Now this causes **repulsion** when a magnet brought closer.
This then leads to **locomotion**, we call this effect the motor - ooh.

When a **current** carrying wire is placed in a field it feels a force, a force created.
Take these **three factors** to cal-cu-late it.

We just need the left-hand rule.
First finger is field it's cool.
Second current of course.
That then makes your **thumb** the force.

Science skills

Demonstrating the magnetic field around a wire

You can put a wire through a horizontal piece of card.

While a current is flowing, use a plotting compass to draw the magnetic field around the wire.

You can use the right-hand grip rule to find the direction of the magnetic field.

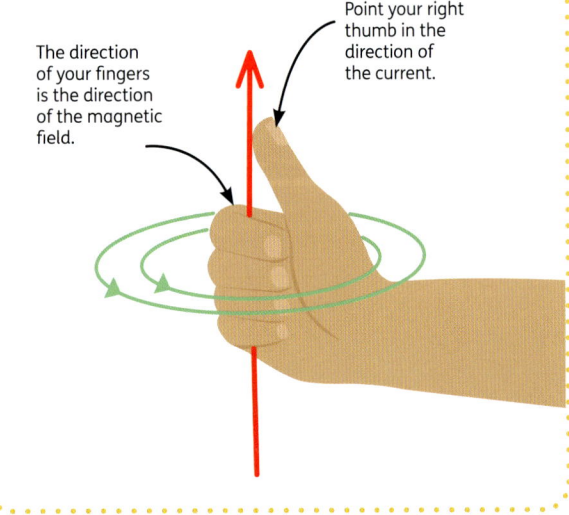

The direction of your fingers is the direction of the magnetic field.

Point your right thumb in the direction of the current.

Magnetic field around a wire

When a current flows through a conducting wire, a magnetic field is produced around the wire. The strength of the magnetic field depends on the current through the wire and the distance from the wire.

The field lines on the diagram are closest together near the wire, where the field is strongest. They are further apart at a distance from the wire, as the field becomes weaker.

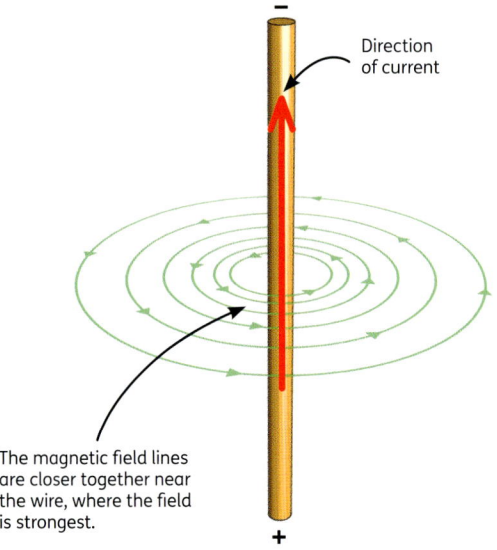

Direction of current

The magnetic field lines are closer together near the wire, where the field is strongest.

Magnetism and Electromagnetism

Solenoids

When you wind a wire into a coil, the strength of the magnetic field created by a current through the wire increases. The coil is called a solenoid. The magnetic field inside a solenoid is strong and uniform.

The magnetic field around a solenoid has a similar shape to that of a bar magnet. Adding an iron core increases the strength of the magnetic field of a solenoid. An electromagnet is a solenoid with an iron core.

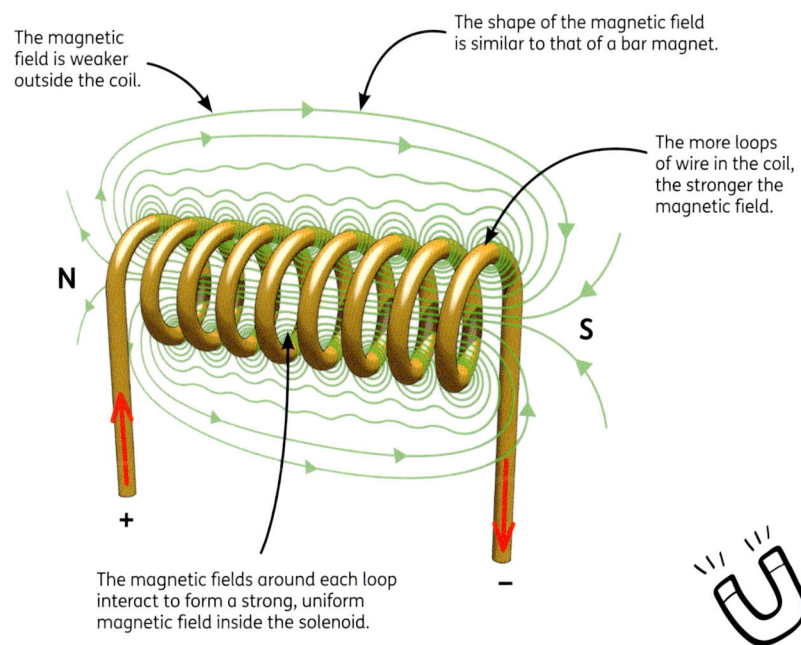

Using electromagnets

Relays
A relay is an electrical switch. A small electric current is used to turn on another circuit that has a larger current.

The ignition circuit in a petrol car uses a relay. The key is in the low-current part of the device. The high-current part starts the motor.

Separating metals
Electromagnets are used in scrap yards to separate magnetic materials from other metals.

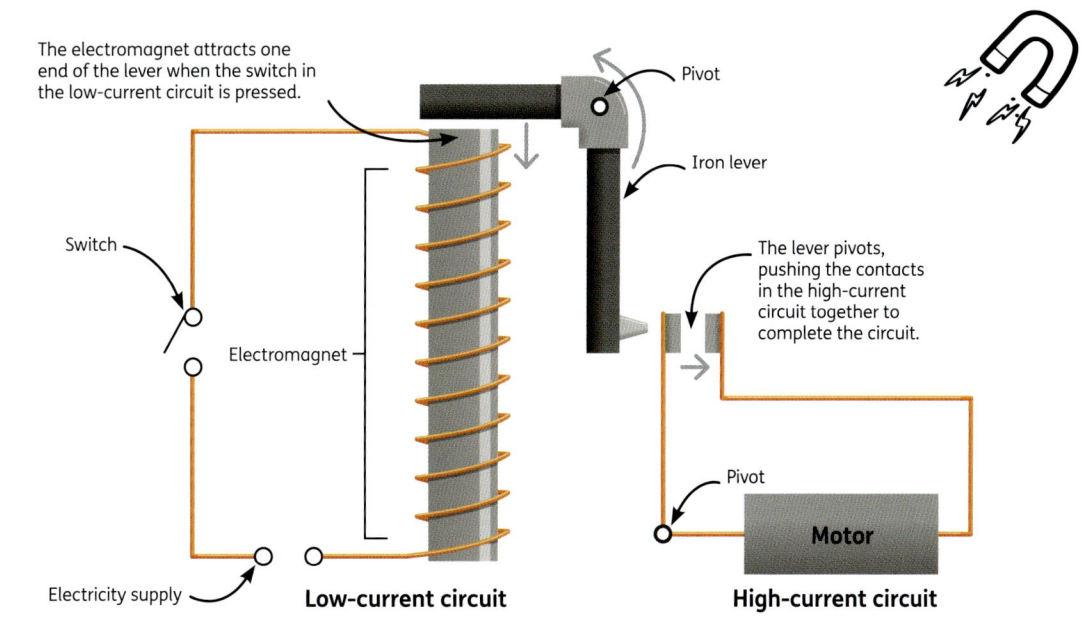

Magnetism and Electromagnetism Recap Quiz

 Find a pen and paper and work through these revision questions.

1. Explain the difference between permanent and induced magnets.
2. What is a magnetic material?
3. What type of force do magnets exert on each other?
4. Define "magnetic field".
5. Describe how to plot the magnetic field pattern of a bar magnet using a compass.
6. Explain how the strength of the magnetic field around a current-carrying wire can vary.
7. Where is the magnetic field of a magnet strongest?
8. Explain how to find the direction of a magnetic field in a wire.
9. What is a solenoid?
10. How do you increase the strength of the magnetic field in a solenoid?
11. State two uses of electromagnets.
12. State how an electromagnet could be used in a scrap yard.

Check your answers on page **110**.

Space Physics

At the end of this chapter, you should be able to:

- ✓ Describe what the Solar System is made up of.
- ✓ Explain how fusion reactions keep a star in equilibrium.
- ✓ Describe the life cycles of stars similar to the Sun and much more massive than the Sun.
- ✓ Explain how elements heavier than iron are formed.
- ✓ Describe the orbits of planets, moons and artificial satellites.
- ✓ Explain what red-shift is.
- ✓ Explain that the change of each galaxy's speed with distance is evidence of an expanding Universe.
- ✓ Explain how red-shift provides evidence for the Big Bang model.

Space Physics

The Solar System and Stars

> ### Key facts
> - The Solar System has eight major planets, minor planets, asteroids and comets all orbiting the Sun.
> - There are two main paths for the life cycle of stars, which depend on the star's mass.

Solar System

Our Solar System is a small part of the Milky Way galaxy and has:
- One star – the Sun.
- Eight major planets – from the Sun outwards: Mercury, Venus, Earth, Mars, Jupiter, Saturn, Uranus and Neptune.
- Dwarf planets beyond Neptune, including Pluto.
- Comets and asteroids.

Moons are natural satellites that orbit planets.

Asteroids are small rocky bodies that are mostly between Mars and Jupiter.

All stars form in nebulas – giant clouds of gas and dust.

A pocket of gas contracts to form a dense, spinning clump, eventually triggering nuclear fusion in the core.

Massive star

When a massive star runs out of fuel, it swells to form a supergiant.

Average-sized star

As an average-sized star runs out of fuel, it swells to form a red giant.

The life cycle of a star

A star goes through a life cycle. The life cycle is determined by the size of the star. The diagram shows the life cycle for a star about the size of the Sun and a star that is much more massive than the Sun.

At the start of a star's life cycle, dust and gas are drawn together by gravitational attraction to form a **protostar**. Eventually fusion starts. This is how the Sun was formed.

Stellar equilibrium

Gravity is always trying to pull a star inwards and collapse it. The energy from fusion reactions tries to push the star outwards.
A star is stable as long as these two forces are balanced, or in **equilibrium**.

Dwarf planets

Dwarf planets, such as Pluto, are objects that have enough mass to form a spherical shape, but not enough to clear their orbits of other material.

Moons

Moons orbit planets. There are more than 200 moons in the Solar System. Most of them orbit major planets.

Comets

Comets are a mix of ice and rock. They have long, elliptical orbits. They often develop long bright tails as they travel close to the Sun.

Asteroids

Asteroids are usually made of rock and metal left over from the formation of planets. They are irregular in shape. Most of them orbit the Sun in a belt between the orbits of Mars and Jupiter.

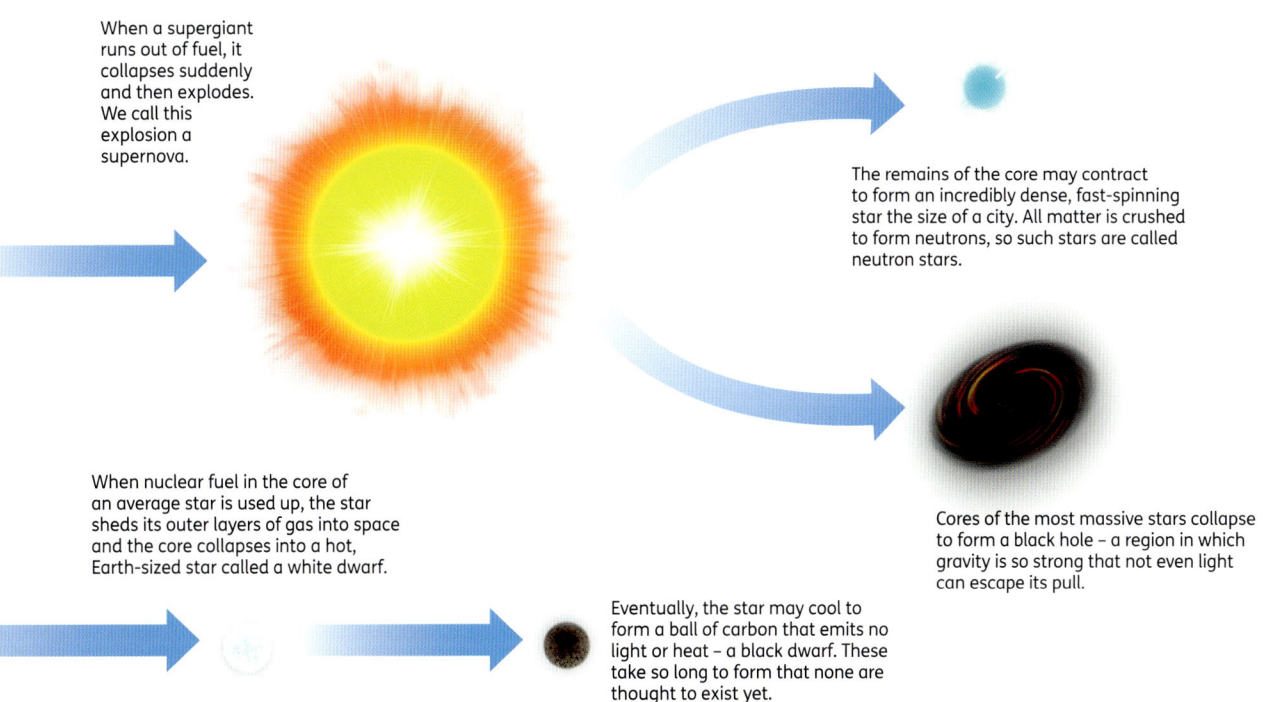

When a supergiant runs out of fuel, it collapses suddenly and then explodes. We call this explosion a supernova.

The remains of the core may contract to form an incredibly dense, fast-spinning star the size of a city. All matter is crushed to form neutrons, so such stars are called neutron stars.

When nuclear fuel in the core of an average star is used up, the star sheds its outer layers of gas into space and the core collapses into a hot, Earth-sized star called a white dwarf.

Cores of the most massive stars collapse to form a black hole – a region in which gravity is so strong that not even light can escape its pull.

Eventually, the star may cool to form a ball of carbon that emits no light or heat – a black dwarf. These take so long to form that none are thought to exist yet.

Forming elements

The main source of energy in stars is hydrogen fusing to make helium. When the hydrogen runs out, helium fuses to make larger elements. In a red giant, helium fuses to make carbon. In a red supergiant, fusion continues to make heavier elements such as nitrogen, oxygen and iron. The largest element that can be made by fusion in a star's core is iron.

Elements heavier than iron are formed in a supernova. A supernova spreads the elements throughout the universe.

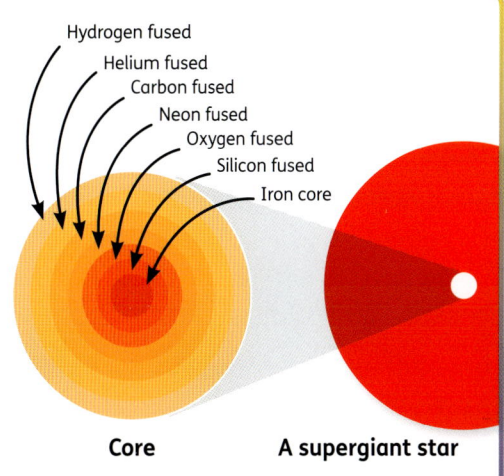

Core — A supergiant star

Orbital Motion and Red-shift

Key facts

- Gravity provides the force that allows planets and both natural and artificial satellites to maintain their circular orbits.
- **Red-shift** provides evidence that the Universe is expanding and supports the **Big Bang theory**.

Orbital motion and satellites

A **natural satellite** is anything that orbits a planet that has not been made by humans. An **artificial satellite** is anything that orbits another body and has been made by humans.

The orbits of planets are nearly circular but the orbits of comets are elliptical.

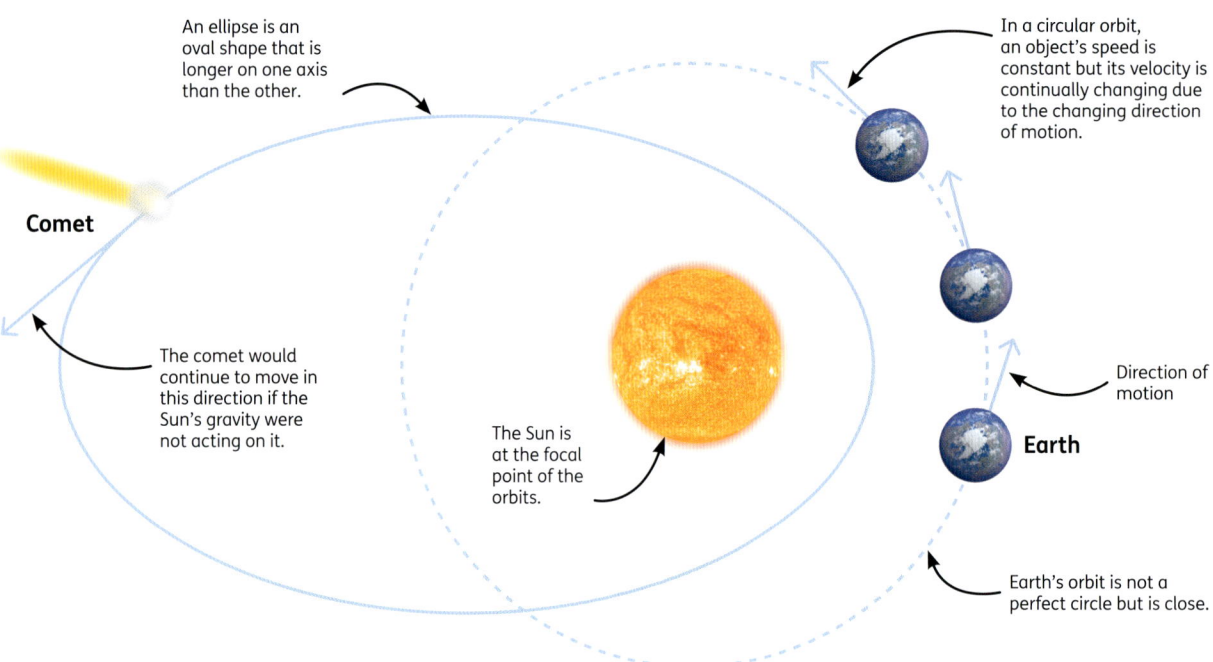

Earth orbits

Different Earth orbits are used for different purposes.

Geostationary orbits are used for weather and communications satellites. A satellite in geostationary orbit stays above the same point on the equator and matches Earth's period of rotation.

Polar orbits are used for Earth-monitoring satellites. A satellite in a polar orbit travels around the planet from pole to pole. They pass over different parts of the planet with each orbit because Earth rotates beneath them.

Low-earth orbits are used for satellites like the International Space Station.

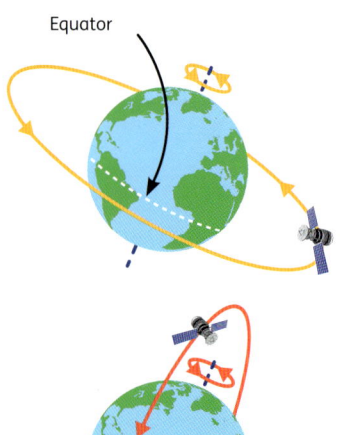

Red-shift

Red-shift is the observed increase in the wavelength of light from most distant galaxies. The further away the galaxies, the faster they are moving and the bigger the observed increase in wavelength.

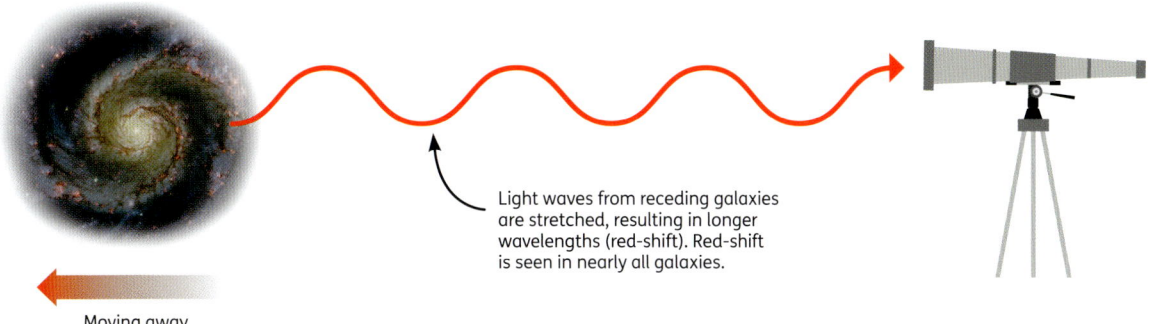

Light waves from receding galaxies are stretched, resulting in longer wavelengths (red-shift). Red-shift is seen in nearly all galaxies.

Moving away

The diagram shows how the lines in the spectrum of light from a distant galaxy are red-shifted when compared with the lines in the spectrum of light from the Sun.

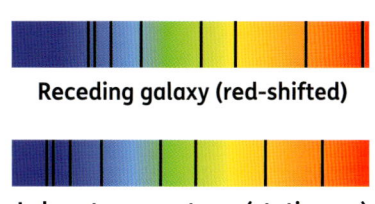

Receding galaxy (red-shifted)

Laboratory spectrum (stationary)

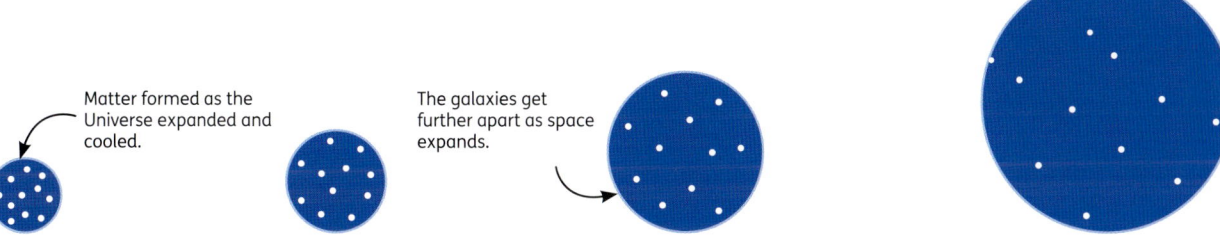

Matter formed as the Universe expanded and cooled.

The galaxies get further apart as space expands.

Big Bang theory

The Big Bang theory suggests that the Universe began from a very small region that was extremely hot and dense about 13.8 billion years ago.

Since 1998 onwards, observations of supernovae suggest that distant galaxies are receding ever faster. The change of each galaxy's speed with distance is evidence that the Universe is expanding. It supports the Big Bang theory.

Cosmic microwave background radiation
Cosmic microwave background radiation is a weak radio signal that is all over the sky. It was predicted by the Big Bang theory and provided evidence to support it.

Dark mass and dark energy

There is still much about the Universe that is not understood. Scientists have not found evidence of dark mass and dark energy.

Content of the Universe

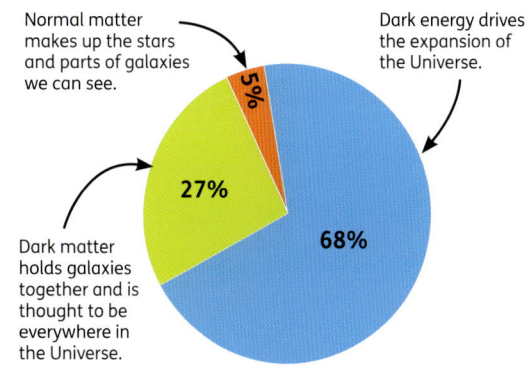

Normal matter makes up the stars and parts of galaxies we can see.

Dark energy drives the expansion of the Universe.

Dark matter holds galaxies together and is thought to be everywhere in the Universe.

5%
27%
68%

Brain Booster

Space Physics Recap Quiz

 Find a pen and paper and work through these revision questions.

1. Name the main components of the Solar System.
2. Describe a protostar.
3. How are elements heavier than iron formed?
4. Describe what happens when a star that is much larger than the Sun runs out of hydrogen.
5. Explain the difference between a natural satellite and an artificial satellite.
6. Describe the similarities and differences in the orbits of comets and the Earth.
7. Explain what red-shift is.
8. Describe the evidence to support the Big Bang theory.

Check your answers on page **110**.

Answers

Energy — 18

1. Energy is transferred by electricity from the chemical energy store of the battery. Energy is then transferred by light and heating to the thermal energy store of the surroundings.
2. The law of conservation of energy states that energy cannot be created or destroyed. It can only be transferred from one store to another.
3. 14.7 J (0.75 × 9.8 × 2)
4. 0.3125 J (0.5 × 250 × (0.20 − 0.15)^2)
5. 1.125 × 10^8 J (0.5 × 250,000 × 30^2)
6. a) Energy transfers by light and sound
   b) Energy transfer by heating
   c) 30 W (2 + 10 + 18 J/s)
   d) 40 per cent (12 ÷ 30 × 100 per cent)
7. By reducing unwanted energy transfers, e.g. in houses by using insulation or thicker walls.
8. A renewable energy resource is one that will not run out. It is being replenished as it is being used.
9. Any two from: solar power, wind power, hydroelectricity, tidal power, biofuels and geothermal.

Electricity — 34

1. a) Circuit diagram with correct symbols for two cells, a switch and a bulb connected in a single loop.
   b) Ammeter should be connected in series with the bulb. Voltmeter should be connected in parallel across the bulb.
2. Correct symbols for a thermistor and an LED – see page 20.
3. Circuit diagram with power supply/cells switch, ammeter and wire connected in a single loop. No set symbol for wire and crocodile clips, but these should be labelled. Voltmeter connected in parallel across the wire.
4. 288,000 J (40 × 2 × 60 × 60)
5. Earth: green and yellow; live: brown; neutral: blue
6. Earth wire provides a route for current to flow to Earth and stops the appliance becoming live.
7. a) 90C (0.05 × 30 × 60)
   b) 20,700 J or 20.7 kJ (90 × 230)
8. Step-up transformers are used at power stations to increase the voltage before transmitting energy through the National Grid. Step-down transformers are used near the consumer to decrease the voltage.
9. By rubbing an insulator with a cloth or rubbing two insulators together, electrons are transferred from one material to the other.
10. See left-hand diagram on page 33.

Particle Model of Matter — 44

1. Liquid
2. Measure the mass of a measuring cylinder using a balance. Add a known volume of liquid to the measuring cylinder and find its mass. Subtract the mass of the empty cylinder from the mass of the cylinder and liquid. Use the density equation to calculate density.
3. 800 kg/m^3 (60 ÷ (2 × 0.05 × 0.75))
4. The internal energy of an object is the total kinetic energy and potential energy of all the particles in the object.
5. The kinetic energy of the particles increases, so its internal energy increases.
6. Specific heat capacity is the amount of energy needed to change the temperature of 1 kg of the material by 1°C, whereas specific latent heat is the amount of energy needed to change the state of 1 kg of the material.
7. a) 2,110 J/k°C (94,950 ÷ (2.5 × 18))
   b) 835,000 J or 835 kJ (2.5 × 334,000)
8. The molecules of a gas are constantly moving in random directions. In a container, the gas particles collide with the walls of the container constantly. Each collision exerts a force that creates pressure.
9. 0.5m^3 (1.5 × 150,000 ÷ 450,000)

Atomic Structure — 58

1. $^{39}_{19}$K
2. An isotope is an atom of an element that has the same number of protons but a different number of neutrons.
3. In the plum pudding model there is a ball of positive charge with negative electrons embedded in it, but in the nuclear model there is a small positively charged nucleus with electrons orbiting the nucleus in different energy levels.
4. a) $^{222}_{86}$Rn → $^{218}_{84}$Po + $^{4}_{2}$He
   b) $^{137}_{55}$Cs → $^{137}_{56}$Ba + $^{0}_{-1}$e
5. a) alpha particle
   b) beta particle
6. 6 hours (activity halves after 6 hours)
7. Background radiation is radiation that is all around us. It is present all the time and comes from natural and artificial sources.
8. Alpha particles
9. Any two of: sterilising surgical instruments, diagnosing cancer and other conditions; treating cancer.
10. In a controlled chain reaction only one neutron goes on to cause another fission. In an uncontrolled chain reaction all the neutrons go on to cause another fission.

Forces — 82

1. A scalar has only magnitude but a vector has both magnitude and direction.
2. 50 N to the left
3. 400 N (50 × 8)
4. 735 N (75 × 9.8)
5. Elastic deformation happens when you stretch an object, such as a spring, and release it and it returns to its original shape. Inelastic deformation happens when you stretch a material and release it and it does not return to its original shape.

6. The number of air molecules above a surface decreases as the height of the surface above ground level increases. The weight of air above you decreases with increasing height.
7. Find the gradient. Draw a right-angled triangle under the graph. Use the triangle to find change in distance and change in time. Divide change in distance by change in time to find speed.
8. Travelling at a constant velocity
9. 0.75 m/s² ((40 − 10) ÷ 30)
10. According to Newton's first law the car will continue to move at the same velocity – that is, at the same speed and in the same direction.
11. There are two pairs: the force of the person on the chair and the force of the chair on the person; the pull of the Earth on the person and the pull of the person on the Earth.
12. Stopping distance is the sum of the thinking distance and braking distance. Thinking distance is the distance travelled in the time a person takes to react to a hazard such as applying the brakes. Braking distance is the distance travelled from when the brakes are applied to when the vehicle comes to a stop.
13. Any three from: tiredness, drugs, alcohol and distractions, such as trying to use a mobile phone.

Waves 96

1. The vibrations in a transverse wave are at right angles to the direction the wave travels. The vibrations in a longitudinal wave are parallel to the direction the wave travels. Transverse waves can travel through a vacuum but longitudinal waves cannot.
2. The amplitude of a wave is the maximum displacement of a point on a wave away from its undisturbed position.
3. 8 m/s ((8 ÷ 5) × 5)
4. Two people stand at least 100 m apart. The first person makes a noise and the second person starts a stopwatch. When the second person hears the noise they stop the stopwatch. Then use the equation Speed = Distance ÷ Time to work out the speed of sound in air. You could also use an echo bouncing off a solid surface like a wall, but the distance needs to be doubled as the sound is travelling to the wall and back.
5. When light enters the glass block at an angle it is refracted/changes direction and bends towards the normal. When it leaves the glass it is refracted/changes direction and bends away from the normal.
6. An electromagnetic wave is a transverse wave that transfers energy. They all travel at the same speed in a vacuum.
7. A matt black surface.
8. Any three from: electrical heaters, for cooking food, infrared cameras and sending signals from a TV remote control to the TV.
9. Ultraviolet radiation can harm skin cells, causing sunburn and can cause skin to age prematurely. There is also an increased risk of cancer and it can damage the retina of the human eye.
10. A blue T-shirt will appear black in green light because it absorbs green light.
11. A red filter absorbs all wavelengths of light except red. It transmits only red light.
12. The image is virtual, upright and diminished.

Magnetism and Electromagnetism 102

1. A permanent magnet produces its own magnetic field. An induced magnet is a material that becomes a magnet when it is placed in a magnetic field.
2. A magnetic material can be made into a magnet or will be attracted to a magnet.
3. Non-contact
4. The region around a magnet where a force acts on another magnet or on a magnetic material.
5. Place the plotting compass near the north pole of the magnet. Draw a dot at the end of the needle away from the magnet. Move the plotting compass so that the other end of the needle is where you drew the dot. Repeat until the plotting compass is at the other pole of the magnet. Draw a smooth curve to connect all your dots. Repeat for other starting points at the pole of the magnet.
6. The strength of the magnetic field varies with the distance from the wire and the size of the current through the wire.
7. Near the poles.
8. Right-hand grip rule: thumb direction of current, direction of fingers is direction of magnetic field.
9. A coil of wire
10. Add an iron core to the solenoid. (It can also be increased by increasing the number of turns and the current in the coil.)
11. Relay and separating materials
12. Separate magnetic and non-magnetic materials, hold on to magnetic material while on, drop material into container when off.

Space Physics 108

1. The eight planets (Mercury, Venus, Earth, Mars, Jupiter, Saturn, Uranus and Neptune), dwarf planets (including Pluto), moons, comets and asteroids.
2. A protostar is a dense cloud of dust and gas.
3. In a supernova
4. The star turns into a red supergiant. Fusion starts to create elements larger than helium. When it runs out of fuel, the star collapses suddenly and then explodes in a supernova. The remains then form either a neutron star or a black hole, depending on the mass of the original star.
5. A natural satellite is anything that orbits a planet that has not been made by humans. An artificial satellite is anything that orbits another body and has been made by humans.
6. Both comets and the Earth orbit the Sun. The orbit of the Earth is almost circular but the orbits of comets are elliptical.
7. Red-shift is the observed increase in the wavelength of light from most distant galaxies.
8. Red-shift indicates that the further away a galaxy is, the faster that it is moving away from us. This provides evidence that the Universe is expanding and supports the Big Bang theory. Cosmic microwave background radiation also supports the theory.

Exam Board References

Pages	AQA	Edexcel
6–7	4.1.1.1	3.3, 8.1, 8.2, 8.4
8–9	4.1.1.2	3.1, 3.2, 3.5, 8.8, 8.9
10–11	4.1.1.3	14.8, 14.11
12–13	4.1.1.4	8.12, 8.13, 8.14
14–15	4.1.2.1, 4.1.2.2	3.4, 3.6, 3.7, 3.8, 3.9, 3.10, 3.11, 8.3, 8.10, 8.11, 8.15, 9.10
16–17	4.1.3	3.13, 3.14
20–21	4.2.1.1, 4.2.1.2	10.2, 10.4, 10.5, 10.7, 10.8, 10.9
22–23	4.2.1.3	10.1, 10.11, 10.13, 10.15, 10.16, 10.17
24–25	4.2.1.4	10.12, 10.18, 10.19, 10.20, 10.21, 10.22
26–27	4.2.2	10.3, 10.14
28–29	4.2.3	10.32, 10.33, 10.34, 10.35, 10.36, 10.37, 10.39, 10.41, 10.42
30–31	4.2.4	10.6, 10.28, 10.29, 10.30, 10.31, 10.42, 13.8, 13.9
32–33	4.2.5	11.1, 11.2, 11.3, 11.4, 11.5, 11.6, 11.7, 11.8, 11.9, 11.10
36–37	4.3.1.1	14.1, 14.2, 14.3
38–39	4.3.1.2, 4.3.2.1	14.4, 4.5, 14.6
40–41	4.3.2.2, 4.3.2.3	14.7, 14.8, 14.9
42–43	4.3.3	14.12, 14.13, 14.14, 14.15, 14.16, 14.17, 14.18, 14.19
46–47	4.4.1.1, 4.4.1.2	6.1, 6.2, 6.2, 6.4, 6.5, 6.6, 6.7, 6.8, 6.9, 10.1
48–49	4.4.1.3	6.17
50–51	4.4.2.1, 4.4.2.2	6.10, 6.11, 6.14, 6.15, 6.16, 6.18, 6.19, 6.20, 6.21, 6.22, 6.24
52–53	4.4.2.3, 4.4.2.4	6.23, 6.25, 6.26, 6.27, 6.32
54–55	4.4.3	6.12, 6.13, 6.28, 6.29, 6.30, 6.31, 6.33
56–57	4.4.4	6.37, 6.38, 6.39, 6.40, 6.43, 6.44, 6.45
60–61	4.5.1.1, 4.5.1.2, 4.5.1.3	2.1, 2.2, 2.3, 2.4, 2.16, 2.17, 2.18, 9.1, 9.2
62–63	4.5.1.4, 4.5.2	8.5, 8.6
64–65	4.5.3	15.1, 15.2, 15.3, 15.4, 15.5, 15.6
66–67	4.5.4	9.6, 9.7, 9.8, 9.9
68–69	4.5.5.1, 4.5.5.2	15.7, 15.8, 15.9, 15.10, 15.11, 15.12
70–71	4.5.6.1.1, 4.5.6.1.2	2.6, 2.12
72–73	4.5.6.1.3, 4.5.6.1.4	2.5, 2.7, 2.11
74–75	4.5.6.1.5	2.8, 2.9, 2.10, 2.13
76–77	4.5.6.2.1, 4.5.6.2.2, 4.5.6.2.3	2.14, 2.15, 2.19, 2.23
78–79	4.5.6.3.1, 4.5.6.3.2	2.27, 2.28, 2.30
80–81	4.5.6.3.3, 4.5.6.3.4	2.29, 2.31, 2.32
84–85	4.6.1.1, 4.6.1.2	4.1, 4.2, 4.3, 4.4, 4.5, 4.6
86–87	4.6.1.2	4.7, 4.17
88–89	4.6.1.3	4.9, 4.10, 4.16, 5.1, 5.9
90–91	4.6.2.1, 4.6.2.2	5.7, 5.8, 5.10, 5.11, 5.19
92–93	4.6.2.3, 4.6.2.4, 4.6.2.6, 4.6.3	5.1, 5.11, 5.20, 5.21, 5.22, 5.24
94–95	4.6.2.5	5.4, 5.5, 5.6, 5.15
98–99	4.7.1	12.1, 12.2, 12.3, 12.4, 12.5, 12.6
100–101	4.7.2.1	12.7, 12.8, 12.9
104–105	4.8.1.1, 4.8.1.2	7.2, 7.3, 7.4, 7.5, 7.16, 7.17, 7.18
106–107	4.8.1.3, 4.8.2	7.1, 7.6, 7.7, 7.8, 7.9, 7.10, 7.11, 7.12, 7.13, 7.14, 7.15

Acknowledgments

The publisher would like to thank the following for their kind permission to reproduce their photographs:

(Key: a-above; b-below/bottom; c-centre; f-far; l-left; r-right; t-top)

7 Science Photo Library: GIPHOTOSTOCK (t). **9 Getty Images / iStock:** E+ / Abeleao (cra). **10 Alamy Stock Photo:** D. Hurst (ca/Ice). **Dreamstime.com:** Flas100 (ca/paper); Somchai Somsanitangkul / Tank_isara (ca); Jaroslaw Grudzinski / jarek78 (cra). **Fotolia:** apttone (cr/diamond). **13 Getty Images / iStock:** 3DSculptor (b); E+ / Abeleao (t/x2). **14 Dreamstime.com:** Chukov (bc). **30 Dreamstime.com:** Msphotographic (cr). **31 Shutterstock.com:** Artmim (tr). **32 Science Photo Library:** Martyn F. Chillmaid (br). **37 Dreamstime.com:** Norgal (ca); Petro Perutskyy (cla). **38 Dreamstime.com:** Andreykuzmin (c); Valentyn75 (bl); Nikkytok (crb); Romikmk (br). **39 123RF.com:** Mariusz Blach (crb). **Dreamstime.com:** Mykola Davydenko (cr). **Getty Images / iStock:** E+ / Mlenny (b). **41 Science Photo Library:** Turtle Rock Scientific (cr). **42 Dorling Kindersley:** Gerard Brown / Pedal Pedlar (bl). **Shutterstock.com:** Jaya Bharathi A (cr). **50 Dreamstime.com:** Blackstudiopl (c/texture x2); Potatos (cl/texture). **53 Dorling Kindersley:** Arran Lewis / Zygote (c/x2). **55 Depositphotos Inc:** microgen (cl). **Science Photo Library:** Centre Jean-Perrin (cr, br). **61 Science Photo Library:** Martyn F. Chillmaid (cl). **62 Alamy Stock Photo:** parkerphotography (b). **63 Dreamstime.com:** Paul Prescott / Paulprescott (br). **66 Dreamstime.com:** Lukawo (bl). **67 Dreamstime.com:** Brad Calkins (cr); Andrei Kuzmik (c); Joao Virissimo (cl); Tuja66 (b). **68 Dreamstime.com:** Chernetskaya (bl). **84 Dreamstime.com:** Le Thuy Do (crb). **85 Dreamstime.com:** Gualtiero Boffi (tl). **87 123RF.com:** alexzaitsev (b). **Dreamstime.com:** Kanok Sulaiman (cb). **93 Dreamstime.com:** Lemonsoup Whangchom (cb/balls x3). **98 Dreamstime.com:** Ilonashorokhova (cl/x2); Timawe (bl). **Shutterstock.com:** Yellow Cat (clb). **99 Dorling Kindersley:** Stephen Oliver (b). **106 Dreamstime.com:** Intrepix (cr/x2). **NASA:** SOHO - EIT Consortium, ESA (c). **107 NASA:** ESA, S. Beckwith (STScI), and the Hubble Heritage Team (STScI / AURA) (tl)

Cover images: Front and Back: **Adobe Stock:** miloje (Textured Background); Back: **Dreamstime.com:** Beaniebeagle clb/ (Tubes), Vladimir Gladcov clb, Sergey Kolesov clb/ (Mark), Mex D clb/ (brain), Ylivdesign clb/ (explosion)

About the author

Matt Green, aka The Rapping Science Teacher, is a TikTok sensation, TV broadcaster, author and business owner, famous for his viral rapping science videos across social media.

Thanks to Matt's educational and entertaining videos and his performances of acclaimed freestyles on TV and radio, Matt, the former Head of Chemistry at a London comprehensive school, now has millions of followers across his social media platforms and is a regular guest on primetime TV and radio shows.

Content creator Matt works with many leading brands, and uses his teaching skills to educate and entertain students on social media by releasing 30-second GCSE science rap videos every week, with subjects ranging from respiration to electrolysis, teamed with chart-topping soundtracks.

Matt now brings you three new revision guides with his famous TikTok raps to help you to **Rap. Revise. Remember!**